"There is a vulnerability in rebuilding your faith after an earlier version has collapsed. Kate Boyd shows us that vulnerability with clarity and kindness—and without judgment. *An Untidy Faith* isn't a how-to but a how-I-did, a humble invitation to consider that there's a life of faith after deconstruction for those who seek it."

—**JARED BYAS**, author of *Love Matters More* and cohost of *The Bible for Normal People*

"For those disentangling their faith in the face of church abuse scandals and political idolatry, Kate Boyd offers wise and compassionate guidance for a better path forward. *An Untidy Faith* centers the global church, prioritizes faithful interpretation of Scripture, and clings to Jesus amid the failures of his church. I'm thrilled to have a resource I can confidently give to people asking big and important questions about the Christian faith."

—**KAITLYN SCHIESS**, author of *The Ballot and the Bible: How Scripture Has Been Used and Abused in American Politics* and *Where We Go from Here* and *The Liturgy of Politics: Spiritual Formation for the Sake of Our Neighbor*

"Kate Boyd has written a thoughtful and well-researched book that is helpful for all Christians as we navigate culture and our faith in the midst of it. She guides us all with kindness, facts, biblical truth, and vulnerability. This is a book I will recommend to all who come to me with questions about deconstruction and rebuilding faith in the face of so many questions."

—**KRISTEL ACEVEDO**, spiritual formation director at Transformation Church and author of *3 Big Questions That Shape Your Future*

"*An Untidy Faith* is a book that provides ample space for nuance, asking questions and disentangling from toxic forms of Christianity. Kate Boyd does a beautiful job of writing honestly, passionately, and with conviction about her own journey as well as what she has experienced with others. I particularly love that she doesn't leave you stuck but rather invites you, if you are willing, to journey along with her to construct a meaningful path to faith that makes sense."
—**ROBERT MONSON**, writer, speaker, and codirector of Enfleshed

"Kate Boyd offers a safe seat on the sofa for a truthful and thoughtful discussion about the long-road journey of a living faith in God—and the potholes and detours that have disoriented and disenfranchised people throughout history. No matter where readers are on their faith journey, they will find Kate's wisdom to be encouraging and gracious. She is the friend we all need to keep us focused on what is true and trustworthy."
—**RONNE ROCK**, mentor, speaker, and author of *One Woman Can Change the World: Reclaiming Your God-Designed Influence and Impact Right Where You Are*

"Deconstructing one's faith can be a messy endeavor, leaving a person to wonder whether there is anything left in the rubbish of a religion ruined by divisive politics, questionable ethics, and most of all, the trauma of lost trust. However, Kate Boyd does not leave us in the wreckage of cynicism, but rather offers us the rare commodity of joy. *An Untidy Faith* describes a treasure recovered by the continued life and work of Jesus, one who seeks to build a kingdom within us and around us, in our broken hearts and through community with kindred travelers."
—**PHUC LUU**, PhD, author of *Jesus of the East: Reclaiming the Gospel for the Wounded*

An UNTIDY FAITH

JOURNEYING BACK TO THE JOY OF FOLLOWING JESUS

KATE BOYD

HERALD PRESS

Harrisonburg, Virginia

Herald Press
PO Box 866, Harrisonburg, Virginia 22803
www.HeraldPress.com

Library of Congress Cataloging-in-Publication Data
Names: Boyd, Kate (Bible Teacher), author.
Title: An untidy faith : journeying back to the joy of following Jesus / by Kate Boyd.
Description: Harrisonburg, Virginia : Herald Press, [2023] | Includes
    bibliographical references.
Identifiers: LCCN 2022057219 (print) | LCCN 2022057220 (ebook) | ISBN
    9781513811796 (paper) | ISBN 9781513811802 (hc) | ISBN 9781513811819
    (ebooks)
Subjects: LCSH: Christian life. | BISAC: RELIGION / Christian Living / Spiritual
    Growth | RELIGION / Christian Theology / General
Classification: LCC BV4501.3 .B6955 2023 (print) | LCC BV4501.3 (ebook) |
    DDC 248.4—dc23/eng/20230201
LC record available at https://lccn.loc.gov/2022057219
LC ebook record available at https://lccn.loc.gov/2022057220

Study guides are available for many Herald Press titles at www.HeraldPress.com.

AN UNTIDY FAITH
© 2023 by Kate Boyd.
Released by Herald Press, Harrisonburg, Virginia 22803. 800-245-7894.
    All rights reserved. Published in association with the Books & Such Literary
    Management, 52 Mission Circle, Suite 122, PMB 170, Santa Rosa, CA 95409-
    5370, www.booksandsuch.com.
Library of Congress Control Number: 2022057219
International Standard Book Number: 978-1-5138-1179-6 (paperback);
    978-1-5138-1180-2 (hardcover); 978-1-5138-1181-9 (ebook)
Cover and interior design by Merrill Miller
Printed in United States of America

27 26 25 24 23   10 9 8 7 6 5 4 3 2 1

For Daniel, who walked with me even when we weren't sure where we were going or who we would become along the way

CONTENTS

Foreword

CHRISTIANITY IS NOT new. It may be relatively young as far as belief systems in world history go, but it is not new. In fact, for many of us (particularly in Western contexts), it is the default and primary lens through which we view and interact with the world. So much so that we often fail to examine exactly what it means to be Christian and how that identity influences our existence in the places we've been planted. This reality presents problems in an age when new perspectives are only a click away, waiting to call into question the validity of each of our experiences one by one. *How does our faith survive in a world that expands around us?*

Kate Boyd and I found each other on Twitter. It was October of 2020, in the relative infancy of the COVID-19 pandemic. In an era of social distancing, many people turned to social media as a watering hole of sorts. Kate and I met each other as Christians who are on Twitter and practicing social distancing do: debating about butt bread (though she insisted that the end of a loaf of bread is called the "heel"). And in the time since, I've come to recognize her as something of a kindred spirit (disagreements about bread aside).

We are two people raised in the Christian faith who have grown to appreciate the practice of examining that faith in its many expressions. I see in Kate a beloved sister who is determined to keep Jesus the main thing while letting the other chips fall where they may. In Kate, I sense a seeker who leans into the mystery of a faith in a world to come and how that faith unfolds in the world that is. I see a seeker who revels in the task of constructing a way of being that honors this paradoxical reality. And I do mean revel in the literal sense, for there is an unmistakable joy in her pursuit.

In the pages that follow, we are given a window into that pursuit. I encourage you to lean in as Kate ushers us around the world, pulling at the threads of what many of us have come to know as true. In this book, the threads are not stretched for the sake of destroying our faith. The threads are tugged for the sake of *expanding* our faith. For as we fill ourselves with more experiences and perspectives, we discover that many of the ways of being and belonging we once carried no longer fit us properly. This book offers a companion in the quest of refitting the clothes we wear on the journey.

We do not grow in faith by ignoring or trying to unsee the things that we have seen. We are not stronger for marginalizing the perspectives of those who have lived different lives than we have. There is a freedom that comes in sorting through the experiences we gather and putting them in conversation with the faith that many hold so dearly. There is a joy to be found in the world outside the confines of our own. The journey of disentangling need not be an exercise in despair. There is liberty in following Jesus, and pleasant rest to be found where he leads. My prayer is that in *An Untidy Faith*, you find belonging in new places.

> —R. G. A. "Trey" Ferguson III, founding president at RFX Ministries, director of equipping at Refuge Church Miami, and cohost of *Three Black Men* podcast

Introduction

IT'S TIME TO renew my passport. It's a day that I knew would come, but it still makes me sad. Some people love the idea of a fresh, new one—hearing the slight crackle of the spine as you open it up and feeling the tiny breeze that comes with flipping through the clean pages. Not me, not today, not with my passport.

When you renew your passport, you have to send in the old one. I get a pit in my stomach just thinking about it. It makes me nervous to put something that's been around the world with me into the mail. What if I never see it again? My passport isn't just a booklet with a few stamps in it. It's an old friend. She and I, we've been through some things together, and I don't want to lose her.

Actually, she's more than a friend. She's been my academic advisor. For ten years or so, this blue passport has opened doors to the world and into my faith. I was educated at what I like to call the "passport seminary." My professors were the missionaries and faithful believers I encountered on the ground around the world. My textbooks were their stories and the Bible. Most people go to seminary to learn how to be leaders in the church. At the passport seminary, I learned I already was a leader in the church. I just had to figure what that meant for where I am.

Because of that passport, I've become a new kind of Christian. Seeing how Jesus and the church came alive in the lives of believers around the world shook my faith to its core, and in doing so, it shook away all the things I had added to my faith that weren't necessary. I was pushed out of my comfort zone and forced to examine everything I believed. On the other side of the world, I discovered I'd been duped into a version of faith that didn't seem big enough for my experiences there. And I was angry.

Perhaps you are reading this because you've been there too, or because you're there now. You're not alone. This is normal. This is healthy, even though it hurts. This isn't a punishment but an invitation to wrestle with a kind of cultural Christianity shaped by American evangelicalism. If you're willing to wrestle, then this book is for you.

The more I wrestled, the more I found that God's vision for us is still compelling, that Jesus is still worth following, and that there's a way to practice our faith that leads to the flourishing of the world. If you'll permit me, I'd love to be your tour guide through two journeys that changed how I believe and practice my faith in community.

The Journey Back to Belief in the Church

When your eyes begin to open to see some of the ways American evangelicalism has been culpable and complicit in some of the worst parts of American history, the first question you inevitably ask is: Is Christianity even good? Is it something I even want to be part of? As we'll see, I found the answer by looking beyond my own personal and local contexts into the history of the church and its current global expressions. There I discovered that the mission is still better than the mistakes of the people along the way. On our first journey, we'll wrestle the big picture beliefs of Christianity out of the hands of a dominant church culture in America that attempts to define these beliefs on its own terms.

The Journey into Joyful Practice

After you settle the first question, you then have to ask: how do I take hold of God's vision and put it into practice on this earth right now? I know that when you're wrestling with these big questions it can feel lonely—when you see what can be, it can be harder to accept what currently is. On our second journey, we will begin to diagnose the ways we may have missed the mark in how we practice the faith together, then discover how to reclaim God's vision for God's community and how to live into our place in that community with joy.

Inside these pages are some of the stories of people and places that changed my life. They're spread across five continents, and you won't know their exact names or locations. But you'll know their hearts and see a sliver of their lives like I did. Through this journey, I think you might discover what's in your heart, too, and find that God can handle the reexamining of your faith.

We need not be afraid of becoming new people. The invitation into life with Christ is one of constant reformation. Transformation comes with the territory. If you're willing to take these journeys with me, I hope you begin to find joy in the wandering and wrestling, because in many ways, the process is the point. It's in the process that we become the people that go beyond believing and begin to act in accordance with what we find to be true. Looking back, I think you'll see God was with you in every doubt, question, and decision—using them to shape you into who you've become. In a few years, we may both return to these pages and see we need to update our beliefs because they have shifted again. And when you do, I hope you'll feel deep relief, like the kind you get when you've finished your last final at the close of a semester, knowing that you've learned a lot about yourself and the subject matter along the way.

I'm offering you a ticket. If you love Jesus but you're feeling distant from his people, this could be the journey you need. It's the trip of a lifetime. Faith required. Passport optional. It's uncomfortable, but it's also thrilling. And don't worry about your baggage. There's plenty of space, and we'll even unpack some of it together. I'll be here to hold your hand while we take off and walk with you as we go. This is the journey we were made for.

Part One

JOURNEY BACK TO BELIEF

ONE

Choose Your Own Deconstruction

I FELT ROBBED. As I stepped off the airplane back home at DFW airport and slowly made my way through the customs line, I was sleep-deprived and sad. I couldn't stop thinking about the people I had encountered and how my experience of Christianity felt both less joyful and less faithful. There's a word in missions circles for this experience: reentry. And it was hitting me so hard it almost knocked me over and made me wonder what I had even spent my life doing.

Ever since I was young, I loved church. I remember memorizing John 3:16 in Sunday school in second grade and pretending to preach from a red-letter Bible (before I could even really read it) at my living room coffee table. I started attending a private Christian school affiliated with a Southern Baptist church in fourth grade, and that's when I began to subscribe to the "good Christian girl" ideal that I would spend many years perfecting. I read the Bible daily, prayed often, followed all the rules of modesty and purity culture, and made A's on my tests in Bible class. I loved Jesus too, but I mostly spent my days trying to get it all just right. I thought I was all in. God was my jam, and even though I had all that knowledge and experience behind me, I felt like I had missed something important, because although my faith was strong it rarely led me out of my cozy and convenient comfort zone.

I had just spent ten days in Latin America with the international church planting organization I worked for. I worked as their writer and eventually their marketing manager, and part of my job was to take documentary trips to the regions we worked in and capture stories on the ground of the work that was happening. It meant long days, sitting very still and listening to people tell how God had changed their lives and was moving through the people and home churches planted in these areas. Miracles were not out of the ordinary, and neither was extraordinary sacrifice or service. In the country I just returned from, you weren't allowed to share the gospel in public or build new church buildings. The government made the practice of Christianity difficult from the outside, forcing certain cells of it to get creative and even bold.

Benita was like that.[1] When my friends that lived and ministered in the area first met her, she was a dedicated member of the Communist Party, which held the power in her neighborhood at the time. That meant she held the government's line when it came to Christianity—nothing new was to be done. No new buildings and no sharing of the faith in public; that was what she knew and that was what she enforced. If someone came into the neighborhood and didn't obey these rules, it was her job to report them to the powers that be. But in one day, everything changed for her.

The night before, Benita woke up sweating. This was not so unusual for summers in her part of Latin America, but the restless feeling she had was. As a mother and grandmother, she wasn't used to feeling this out of control. She took a deep breath, then felt a prompting in her mind: *Fill it with water.*

Her petite home had an outer courtyard that functioned like a front yard, though it was roughly the size of an office. Beyond the teal stone wall and white iron gate was a pool hardly larger than a bathtub, though it was deeper. Dripping with sweat and still in her nightclothes, Benita walked to the pool and began to fill it, not knowing why.

The next day, the restless feeling persisted. She found herself pacing back and forth along her concrete floor, wondering if she was crazy. She knew she was waiting, but she didn't know why until they knocked on her door.

They were a strange pair—the American and the local translator. One young, one older. One tall, one short. But Benita knew they were here to tell her something. She invited them in and listened as they told her about Jesus over small teacups full of hot coffee. By the time they finished, she was in tears. She wasn't even sure why. There was something about the story they told about Jesus. It gave her a hope she didn't have before. She wanted something to live for instead of her life of merely existing and enforcing. When they asked if she wanted Jesus to be Lord of her life, she couldn't say yes fast enough.

Once they prayed that prayer so familiar to us but brand new to her, almost instinctively, she walked outside to the pool she had filled the night before. As she stepped into the heat of the Latin American sun, a salty breeze lifted her hair. The American and the translator followed her outside. Right then and there, she was baptized, and that afternoon she joined in the proclamation of Jesus throughout her neighborhood.

What Benita didn't realize that day was that the Holy Spirit had conspired with her and for her in pursuit of that moment. The nudge she felt the night before, the willingness to open the door, the instinct to move to the pool, and the joyful declaration of Jesus—they were all the Holy Spirit working in her life. And that was just the beginning for her.

I met her about three years later, and she told me how after that moment of baptism, she took her badge, marched over to the party headquarters, and quit on the spot. She knew she couldn't have two competing allegiances. Now she was part of the Christian community that she was meant to report. Her decision cost her a lot—her friends, her job, and her reputation in the neighborhood. But it didn't matter to her.

The day I sat across from her on her light pink couch—holding a tiny cup of very delicious coffee in my hands—she was beaming. For Benita, following Jesus had been worth it. Her family and a few neighbors have come to believe, and they worship together in her home, quietly so as to not attract too much attention. She works for a local government official, and just the week before she had the boldness to share the gospel with him. Every week, she goes to the hospital to keep company with the sick. When I asked her how she made time for all this, or even had the bravery given the circumstances, she said, "It's what Jesus told us to do."

I came of age in the era of "WWJD?" ("What Would Jesus Do?") bracelets. It was a time that we learned to ask the question but settle for answers that made us comfortable. I knew the Sunday school answers, and I spent several days a week at church. And yet, in that short sentence, Benita had challenged me more than I had been challenged in years. She arranged her life around service to Christ instead of her service of Christ around her life. My faith was tidy, checked all the right boxes, and participated in all the right activities. Her faith was messy, inconvenient, and sometimes dangerous. There were no neat compartments and no color-coordinated calendars. She gave up her time, her money, and her space to live like Jesus—and I walked away envying that way of living because her faith was so vibrant.

That little phrase rolled around in my head for weeks. Was it really that simple? Why did it feel like my experience didn't quite line up with that? Why did I feel robbed of knowing Jesus and community the way she did? Why did it seem like God wasn't at work the same way in my life?

All I knew now was that I had stepped off the airplane and back into my homeland, but everything felt different. I didn't feel at home anymore, and I wasn't sure I wanted to. Not if home felt like something less than what God's vision for life was meant to be.

And it wasn't just seeing God at work in other places that drove a wedge between me and the church. It was the church itself. Growing up evangelical, I knew the rules and I knew the "right" things to believe. But I felt like every day something else revealed itself that showed me that the church that had raised me didn't seem to believe those things. Sex scandals, moral failures, unwillingness to care for the poor, and pushing people who didn't fit the ideal mold to the outskirts of the church. The more I wrestled with Benita's words, "It's what Jesus told us to do," the more I felt myself on the outside looking in.

Why did it seem like the American church was so out of step with how Christians around the world saw their role in living out the message of the gospel? Why did the Christianity I knew suddenly seem hollowed out and less embodied than what I saw in Latin America? And why didn't anyone tell me it was supposed to be different? I was questioning everything. Eventually I found myself asking the question that began a new journey in my faith life: What happens when you have new experiences that change how you see the people of God and your place in it?

Enter: Deconstruction

I know *deconstruction* is a buzzword now, but when I was going through it ten years ago, I didn't have the adequate vocabulary to describe this process of questioning things I once held firm. I just felt lost and alone. I wondered why I seemed to be the only person who cared about these differences in belief and practice. I didn't even know how to talk about it with my husband. A barrier was now keeping me from fully engaging with the church, and I realized I had a decision to make.

It's the same one we all have to make at some point, really. Countless others have made it before and after I did. It was time to deconstruct what I thought I knew so I could figure out how to move forward.

Deconstruction is a mindset as much as a process. It requires a willingness to hold everything you believe— regardless of past or present certainty—in your hands with open fingers as you examine it, knowing some of it will fall through the gaps. It is also a process full of tension and tentative steps as you move forward, recontextualizing your faith and its accompanying beliefs and actions with the information you have today.

It's scary to start, and not just for you but for those who have spent their careers telling you what to think. To question the ideas is to question the authority of those who hand them down and all the resources that have been created to keep you on track. When life as they know it or their livelihood is on the line, it becomes easy to put a wall up and a foot down. One question can lead to another and another, and it may just unravel everything.

Though deconstruction seems to be part of the popular lexicon today, it wasn't always such a buzzword in the faith world. The term was first introduced in the 1960s in philosophy by Jacques Derrida as a way of examining the language and logic of literary texts. By the 1980s this gave way to examining these dynamics in nature and society including in areas like law, feminism, film, history, and theology.[2] Postmodernism was making its way into the world, and the original form of deconstruction was helping.

In 2003, author and public theologian Brian McLaren wrote an article for *Leadership Journal,* an evangelical publication for pastors and church leaders, outlining the changes this postmodern stream of thought could bring to how Christianity traditionally expressed itself.[3] He was hopeful, but soon more conferences and articles about the challenges presented by postmodernism, especially with regard to staking a claim for specific and absolute truths about Jesus, began to appear in evangelical circles. Though some of the leaders involved in these endeavors saw deconstruction as a potential ally to one's faith, a fear that it could be carried all the way to universalist beliefs made other Christian leaders uncomfortable.[4]

While addressing postmodernism was a concern for academics and theologians, the term deconstruction hadn't hit the mainstream just yet. When it did, it had taken on a new meaning in Christian circles, thanks to popular teachers like Richard Rohr, who wrote about the opportunity of postmodernism and described faith development as a pattern of construction, deconstruction, and reconstruction.[5] It was no longer a term strictly used in academic disciplines. It was now a way people began to identify where they were in their faith journey. I first remember hearing the word used this way around 2017. Much like its philosophical predecessor, the questions it raised and the doubts it allowed people to explore made many uncomfortable or outraged, but it didn't stop deconstruction from taking the spotlight, especially on social media.

Before we knew it, it seemed like well-known Christians were announcing changes in beliefs or leaving behind their faith altogether as a result of a deconstruction process, and many evangelical institutions and leaders cast them down from their platforms. Popular blogger Jen Hatmaker caught heat as she announced changing beliefs on the morality of homosexuality, leading to her books and Bible studies being pulled from shelves.[6] John Piper famously bid Rob Bell farewell when he published a book with alternative views on hell—being deemed a universalist and having departed from his evangelical upbringing.[7] Lisa and Michael Gungor, who had found success as worship leaders and Grammy-nominated Christian musicians, drifted toward atheism and found themselves in a "critical" posture of faith.[8] Eventually they both determined they were still Christians, even if finding themselves more in Christian mysticism than the mainstream.[9]

Today, because of these kinds of public deconstructions, deconstruction has become less taboo. It might even be considered a niche industry of its own, spinning off popular podcasts and Instagram accounts focused on sorting through current events, church culture, and theology for those who are asking questions.[10]

Growing up in conservative evangelical spaces, I was taught not to question what teachers, leaders, and other adults told me. You believed, and you fought for every doctrine, whether essential or nonessential, gospel or cultural. But I began to question my faith community's culture war approach as I saw famous Christians either changing their minds or failing morally behind the scenes (Bill Hybels, Mark Driscoll, and Ravi Zacharias, to name a few), and eventually the election of Donald Trump, which revealed to me that the "character counts" motto of evangelicals during the Bill Clinton era didn't matter when power was on the line. All together, it caused me and a lot of those around me to take a step back and examine what it is that we believe and if the way we were taught to pursue these ideals actually matched up to what we saw in our leaders and our faith community.

My process of deconstruction started back in Latin America. I couldn't unsee what I saw there and what I had come to recognize about the brand of Christianity I had grown up in. Something had to change. When presented with a moment like this—rife with confusion due to new information and new experiences—I've found people most often make one of three choices for their deconstruction journey: doubling down, demolishing, or disentangling.

Some people choose doubling down. You'll know this person by their dogmatic stances and the defensiveness with which they approach new ideas. Here are a few examples of how someone with a doubling down mindset might react in such situations:

- They immediately label new information in front of them as a threat to the gospel and perhaps call those who have presented the offending idea to "just preach the gospel."

- They create a label for the threat and use it as a buzzword to scare people away.

- They retreat to sources with which they're comfortable, creating an echo chamber that doesn't challenge their old ideas.

Anything that could threaten even a small bit of their worldview gets filtered out as inherently bad. New information gets ignored or dismissed because it doesn't fit in the box they've built for their beliefs. There's a comfort in the doubling down approach. You get certainty, a comfort I understand—I longed for that so much (and in some moments I still do). But when what I had seen didn't match up to the certainty I'd been taught, I knew this approach couldn't provide a way forward for me.

The next option is demolishing. This one is very popular too, and I don't blame people for choosing it. When you feel betrayed and hurt—and many people actually were betrayed and hurt by church leaders or members—it makes sense to want nothing to do with the people and institutions that

hurt you. We have seen a demolishing approach from people like Josh Harris, author of purity culture classic *I Kissed
Dating Goodbye*;[11] Rhett and Link, popular YouTubers;[12] and
Marty Sampson, musician with Hillsong.[13] Often those with
a demolishing mindset say things like:

- "I've seen too much to stay."

- "I don't know if I can believe in a God/church/religion
  that commits or excuses abuse or only cares about maintaining power and privilege."

- "I can't be part of something that's hurt so many people."

I've said some of these things, wondering if it was my time
to exit Christianity. When you find out that your community's beliefs and actions didn't really align after all, anger and
disappointment naturally follow. You start to question if it
was ever true to begin with, and this pain leads you to walk
away. I honestly can't blame people who react this way, given
what they've gone through. It's often a very rational decision
rooted in a painful reality. It gives them freedom to explore
things they didn't feel before, and usually by leaving the
community they grew up in, they find another community
of people who left too—people with whom they can safely
explore these questions.

There's at least one more way, and this is the one I chose.
I chose *disentangling*. Demolishing didn't seem like the right
option to me because I had witnessed the goodness of God
and the church in the world. Though I now recognized the
version of faith I had grown up in as deficient, I decided I
was still in. I still loved Jesus. I felt betrayed by his people, but
Jesus was still such a compelling person and idea to me that I

couldn't help but remain committed. What had changed was the realization that so much of what I thought about Jesus and Christianity was actually tangled up in my American culture. So I set out to separate the two.

As author Carolyn Custis James once wrote, "We need a global conversation because the Bible itself is global."[14] Inspired by that truth and by my encounters abroad, my new motto became, "If it is biblical, it must be global." This decision meant that I had to stop accepting everyone else's word for who Jesus is and what we as the people of God are meant to be, and I had to go look for myself. I had been given the tools, and it was time to use them. I had to let go of my comfortable boxes and give myself space to ask questions and wrestle with doubt and deep thoughts. And I had to make space for the truth that would translate across time and culture.

Disentangling as Discipleship

It turns out that this journey isn't feared or frowned upon by Jesus. When I began to deconstruct all I had been taught, I looked back at the gospels and tried to drop my previous assumptions. As I did, I realized that disentangling is a life-long journey and that it's actually part of the discipleship process. The Holy Spirit, through the Bible and community, is always refining us, peeling away our little idols and false ideas and replacing them with truth and joy in Christ. In fact, I find that Jesus was constantly making space (albeit sometimes in frustration, like in Mark 8 or Matthew 16) for his disciples to figure it out, to let go of their preconceived notions and to see him and his way as the better alternatives that they really are. Throughout his entire journey with his followers, Jesus kept peeling back layers of belief in what it meant to be the Messiah and reorienting his people toward a new way of living.

Whether we do it purposely or not, each of us ends up making God in our own image. We are shaped by more than the Bible. The technology we have, the sheer volume (and content) of the messages we see every day, and the communities in which we live all shape our perceptions of the world around us. As that happens, we start to get ideas about who God is and what God is doing that relate to our own lives. Instead of God shaping our desires, our desires shape our view of God. And wouldn't you know it, the good news becomes what will make each of us happy or successful. But God works on a whole different level than we do. God is telling a grander story, one that includes people in every place and every time, and it was for all our good—physical and spiritual. God's work is for us, and even though God works through us, often God's work looks different from our desires and frequently asks us to sacrifice for others.

Jesus' journey with his disciples often mirrors our own if we're willing to undertake it with him. The disciples came to him with big expectations, and he reshaped their lives with a new vision. Encountering this Jesus will also turn our lives and expectations upside down in the best way as we let him reshape us to let go of our cultural baggage, to love God and love our neighbor more fully.

As a Jewish man raised in the Jewish faith, Jesus knew that the Israelites expected a savior who would swoop in and rescue them from their oppressors to establish their kingdom forever. To them, the idea of the Messiah had a very specific vision attached to it. *Messiah* is derived from a Hebrew root word meaning "to anoint, smear."[15] In its noun forms, it came to be associated with anointed and consecrated sacred spaces and items or people—like kings and priests. Eventually, the idea of the "anointed one" became a source of hope. Another king like David was coming to set Israel back on the path of success.[16] Later on in Jewish tradition, this Messiah ideal would become connected to the "Son of Man," which is a prophecy found in the book of Daniel 7:

> As I watched in the night visions, I saw one like a human being [Son of Man] coming with the clouds of heaven. And he came to the Ancient One and was presented before him. To him was given dominion and glory and kingship, that all peoples, nations, and languages should serve him. His dominion is an everlasting dominion that shall not pass away, and his kingship is one that shall never be destroyed. (Daniel 7:13–14)

Thus the idea of the Messiah became one of a powerful king who would once again establish Israel as a kingdom— one that would not pass away and would carry the authority of God.[17] This idea of the coming king that would restore Israel once and for all was what Peter and others expected of the Messiah, and at every turn, Jesus had to do the work of disentangling those beliefs and expanding the vision from an eternal kingdom of Israel toward an eternal kingdom of God.

Tangle 1: The kingdom of God would be for Israel primarily

Before Jesus walked the earth as a man and introduced a new kind of kingdom, the prevailing belief had been that the good news to come would be for Israel. God's covenant was with Israel, and God gave Israel the Law. Their history was tightly woven to the God of the universe and everything in it. And they were right—it was for Israel, but it was also for everyone.

Jesus spent many days in Gentile territory, and he did the exact same healing and proclaiming of the gospel with them as he did with the Jewish people. Israel is the hook in history and God will keep that covenant, but Jesus flung the door wide open for the rest of us to join in what God is doing. Though it took some time, the disciples would come to see this, and at Pentecost, through them and the Holy Spirit, it would begin to spread.

Tangle 2: The kingdom of God would be for Israel as a nation

Israel had a variety of leaders over the years—prophets, judges, kings, and rulers in exile. The Jewish people dreamed of the coming day when their kingdom would be restored in full after years in exile followed by years of oppression within the Roman empire. Though it seemed as though God had gone silent by not speaking through Israelite prophets, judges, or kings, the people of God clung to the hope that if they kept their end of the deal, they would have the peace and prosperity they dreamed of—the Promised Land would be theirs once more with no outside interference. When Jesus came, the disciples followed him expecting him to become a king who would lead them to victory through revolution. Except Jesus didn't do that. Not only did he not push the national agenda, he didn't seem interested in ruling that way, running away from those who wanted to make him king (John 6).

Jesus taught about a different kingdom, and he showed them what this kingdom looks like in his actions. Instead of leading a big parade, Jesus came into town on a donkey. Instead of being waited on hand and foot, Jesus washed others' feet. In this, he showed the disciples the new rules of the kingdom to come. This is great news for us who are not of Jewish descent because we also get to participate as part of the promised kingdom of God by living in accordance with the way of life God designed for that kingdom. These ideas and ethics are for us to live by and to embody for the world around us so that all might know the love of God. Our allegiance and our agenda are determined by our heavenly King and not by any earthly power. It may conflict with the powers of our day—and in fact the threat this poses to political powers has been the cause of wars across time—but it also connects us to believers everywhere.

Tangle 3: The kingdom of God would be for the elite

Power, money, status—just like any other civilization since the history of forever, these were the defining characteristics of the successful in Jesus' time, even in his own Jewish community that was under Roman rule, and it had become normal and even expected in religious spaces to most value those most valued by society. No matter that God had a tendency of choosing the human you might least expect to be a major part of God's legacy. David, for example, was the youngest in his family, a shepherd not a warrior, and least known of his brothers. Yet it is David that God chooses to become the king of Israel, the model for the anticipated Messiah. Then, like in Jesus' day, no one looked at the lowly little guy in the field as a possible means of re-establishing God's people. It just made sense that those with the right titles, education, and social network would be best positioned to bring Israel back to greatness. So any good leader would focus on the elite, right? But Jesus took a different approach.

Those who were on the outside because of disease or injury or lack of money were the ones that Jesus went to first. Lepers shunned by society? He healed them. Samaritan woman not accepted by her people or the Jews? Jesus talked the longest with her and revealed who he was. Tax collectors, the demon possessed, women in general? He hung out with each of them.

It was the rulers and the rich who often were most challenged by the ways Jesus pushed the boundaries of who matters. In this Jesus modeled a more loving and inclusive vision of what God's people could be. Jesus made way for all of us. He placed no barriers, no hoops, no tests to establish our status. Jesus made God accessible to everyone. The lowly weren't just welcome, they were esteemed. As each of us comes to Jesus flawed and falling short, we find hope in the One who counted us each worthy.

Tangle 4: The kingdom of God would take down Rome

If you're a conquering warrior king, you need an army to lead into revolution. Jesus disappointed the Israelites on both accounts. He didn't recruit fighters. He invited a group of fishermen, tax collectors, and tradesmen into his inner circle and taught them a way of life characterized by love and peace. He traveled around healing, teaching, and feeding people . . . not raising an army. When the empire came for him, he didn't defend himself. In fact, he condemned the violence that was performed on his behalf by Peter (John 18:11). He went willingly into the authorities' hands and was crucified by the empire with the approval of the religious rulers of the day.

The Son of Man did come, and he did create a kingdom that would rule forever. It just looked *nothing* like anyone expected it to. But that's the work of discipleship. It's the slow and steady untangling of what we wish to be true from what is the true will of God. It happens one change at a time, and it doesn't just change your mind but your life.

Once they saw that good news modeled by Jesus, and after his resurrection fully understood what it meant, the disciples spent their life building that kingdom and bringing the spiritual revolution to the physical world. Peter, Thomas, John, and others—most of them went to their death just like their leader. The truth Jesus taught them to fight for meant giving up their power and their lives, and none of us can do that without seriously untangling our own will or our cultural ideas that can strip the power and beauty from the real story. That's part of our life's work.

The Tension of the Christian Life

Growing up, I knew the basic Christian beliefs like the Trinity and the resurrection, but they were often emphasized less than a few hot-button issues that tended to dominate the landscape in my community. I was taught more about the importance of guarding the ideal of the nuclear family and traditional gender roles, putting Christians in places of power (especially where politics are concerned), thinking of stewardship of God's money as how much we have and can get (rather than how we use it for others), and protecting the reputation of the church when it's doing something wrong instead of calling it to repentance. In my disentangling journey, I discovered that much of what I thought was in the camp of *orthodoxy* was actually very tied up with *fundamentalism.*

- *Orthodoxy* is belief in the core doctrines that believers across denominations, borders, and centuries have held to, like belief in the Trinity, that Jesus is fully God and fully man, that his work on the cross provides a way for our salvation, and that he physically rose from the dead.[18]

- *Fundamentalism,* however, may include the above beliefs, but it usually adds to the list a whole lot of other interpretations, regulations, and dogmatic ideologies that aren't necessary to orthodox belief. Fundamentalists give them all equal weight because other non-fundamentalist views could be a "slippery slope" to the wrong kind of church or society.

It might be helpful now to take a few moments to unpack what needs disentangling in your own journey. As you think about your formative experiences in the church, did they look more like orthodoxy or fundamentalism? What issues drew the anger or attention of the pastors and people? Which topics did you hear about the most in sermons and Sunday school classes? Which stances determined who would be "in" and who would be "out"?

Theological conservatives and progressives can both be fundamentalists. Each side has their own list of nonnegotiable beliefs that make them a superior version of Christians and keeps everyone who doesn't agree out. I've been guilty of fundamentalism on both sides too. It's easier to give complete allegiance to a side, to have an "us" and a "them," to have a long bill of cultural items you can check off to ensure ideological purity.

There's safety and comfort in this kind of certainty. What is harder is embracing tension and holding everything up to the light with humility, willing to examine and be examined to find the truth in the tangles. The reality is that though we serve this eternal kingdom that Jesus kept sharing about, we still live in physical ones. Theologians talk about this in terms of the "already" and the "not yet":

- Christ has already come. Christ has not yet come back.

- The world is already moving toward redemption. The world has not yet been fully redeemed.

- We are already wiped clean of our sin. We are not yet incapable of sinning.

- We already possess truth in the word of God and through the Holy Spirit. We do not yet have the capacity to know everything perfectly.

That's where we live. Fundamentalism will ask you to dig in your heels, to go all in on their proposed list of stances (whether conservative or progressive), but disentangling offers a way to move forward that allows you to keep the faith without needing to fit into one box neatly. I knew it would be a challenge to navigate my place on the spectrum of belief while loud voices spoke to me from each end, but I also knew what was important to me and that I wasn't ready to let go of all Jesus had to offer.

The life of a Christian is one of embracing and wrestling with this tension all the time. Part of the work of discipleship is disentangling the truth of the "not yet" from the barriers in the "already." We rarely land on one side of the fundamentalism fence. Embracing this tension doesn't mean you hold nothing to be absolutely true or even that choosing the middle down the line is the right or best choice, but it does mean there are places where you are firm—like orthodox Christian beliefs—and places where you are loose—like approaches to cultural issues or baptism styles that leave space for the less clear points in Scripture. When I put Christ back at the center of my Christianity, I found that I could muster up the courage and hope I needed for the journey even when navigating tension and tricky places.

Disentangling offered me the opportunity to say, "We have gotten things wrong and hurt a lot of people along the way, but I still believe in Christ and his church so much that I'm willing to stay and fight for her."

When I first went to seminary right out of college, I went because I wanted to have the answers to back up my fundamentalism. That's not the reason I would have given at the time. Back then I just knew I wanted answers. I wasn't even sure what the questions were, but I wanted the answers to back up my beliefs. The thing I didn't foresee is that I would be the one asking the questions. I dropped out of seminary for financial reasons back then, and while I didn't get the education I wanted, I got the education I needed.

Benita was among the first of many whom I consider my professors. She didn't know big theological words like *soteriology* and *eschatology*, but she did know Jesus, and the way she lived that out was compelling to me. She gave me the courage to open my Bible and dig deeper so I could take *all* the words of Jesus seriously. She prompted me to start looking at

Christianity as something for every kind of person and not just the few that knew the right things to get mad at.

Because of people like her, the stamps in my passport mean more to me than just evidence of another place I visited. They are the physical reminders of the lessons learned and the inner change I experienced because I had been there. As we take this journey together, I'll share stories of these field professors who showed me a global faith and a bigger Jesus than I had imagined, and cleared the way for the disentangling of my faith that accompanied my physical journeys. These shifts may look like yours, and they may not. But in the end, my desire is that this journey shows you one way to go about this challenging work, and that it continuously calls you back to the Jesus of the Bible and the legacy of the historical and global church. I think you'll find there is still hope to be found within Christianity, and that we can begin to be the bridge of that hope among our own churches and circles of influence.

TWO

Respecting the Bible's Boundaries

SOMEWHERE IN SOUTHEAST Asia between our lodging and that day's headquarters for interviews, I was struggling to find a comfortable spot in my seat. On these trips, we often go to two or three cities over the course of our time in a country, and that means we're sitting in cars for long stretches as we move from place to place. We had been in the SUV so long that I was starting to get a little sore.

But these are the moments where stories are shared and insights are gathered from those you're traveling with. Each of us on the trip—a missionary, a photographer, a translator, and a marketer—had our own collection of places and stories from around the world. As we drove through the countryside, we started talking about how we look at the Bible. The photographer with us started talking about the missionaries he knew in the Middle East, and how they gave him some new insight on the story of Lot.

You have probably heard this biblical story. It's pretty infamous. In Genesis 19, Lot and his family are the only ones being saved from the destruction about to occur in Sodom and Gomorrah. Two angels visit the city, and he invites them into his home. He practically insists, dragging them in because he knows the wicked hearts of the people in the city. Sure enough, the men of the city come knocking on his door demanding the two visitors staying with Lot, and Lot does something most of us could never understand: he offers his daughters instead. This is one of those details that a lot of people skip over because they don't know what to make of it, but my friend explained to us that day that it was actually a misguided act of hospitality.

Every culture I have experienced in Asia, Latin America, and even many in Europe highly prioritizes hospitality in a way North American cultures typically do not. I remember in one South Asian country feeling a bit annoyed because it seemed as though everyone was patronizing me until later a friend described the culture of hospitality that existed there. He shared with me how hospitality would manifest in ways that didn't fit into my notion of American self-sufficiency and independence. This helped me understand that as long as someone there saw me as someone in their care to any extent, they would move mountains to make sure I had all I needed and wanted in their presence. In this way they honor me, and by submitting to their care in those moments, I honor them.

This was a similar value in Lot's culture. Part of the judgment of Sodom and Gomorrah was their treatment of those in need, which would include outsiders who needed shelter for the night (Ezekiel 16:49–50). This is a story of the failures of Sodom, but it is also a story of the failure of Lot among them. Lot could not let his guests be taken advantage of by the men in his city. It was not honorable for them to fall into harm because they were in his care, and he even went above and beyond by volunteering that care and hospitality to them in the first place. So when his neighbors came knocking at his door, Lot did what any good host would do. He protected his guests at all costs. Unfortunately, he did it in a way that would cause the violation of his daughters.

Let's be clear: What Lot does is wrong and horrible. The sexual violence from outside the house in this scene is ungodly, as is the offering of innocent women from inside the house to satiate lust. Learning about the hospitality culture doesn't make light of what Lot does, but it brings some clarity as to why he would even think this a better alternative. Lot responds to competing pressures—caring for his guests and appeasing the aggressive and wicked men at his door. He chooses to compromise rather than stand against the townspeople. He chose poorly.

His uncle Abraham had just argued that Lot and his household were surely good and worth saving, yet we see here an example of the ways that outside pressures compounded on Lot to display his character, which is now found wanting. Through twisted logic, Lot chose the value he wanted to uphold—hospitality above holiness—when he didn't have to leave behind either one. I don't understand the choice he made. I don't think we're supposed to. But I do understand better the pressures that informed his decision that I had never considered before.

It's such a small detail of the story, but seeing it in this new way led me to so many more questions. What had I been missing all this time because I was so far removed from the people of the Bible? Or worse, what might I be reading or teaching poorly because I had put myself, a white American woman, at the center of every verse I read? What did I skip over or not question because I was taught to take someone's word for it?

I had a lot of tools for reading the Bible. I knew how to diagram all the verses and even how to find just the right Scripture reference to point you to the topic you were curious about. But in this moment, I became acutely aware of just how foreign the Bible was to me. I had built my life around what this sacred text says, but what if I didn't actually understand it as well as I thought? What if what is literal for me doesn't make sense when you put it back into its many contexts? What if I was reading my culture into the text more than the text's culture? I had to develop new tools and find new terms for how I interacted with Scripture. And while I found the Bible to be so much richer than I had before, I also found it made my life a little more complicated.

Defining Our Terms

Learning to see the Bible a little differently—and ultimately changing my mind about a few things I accepted as straightforward before—revealed something interesting about the way the Bible, and all the terms we associate with it, had been used in my church culture. In that culture the goal wasn't always objectivity but pushing forward certain narratives. On that list of narratives, biblical inerrancy comes in at number one, and as it turns out, inerrancy as *we* know it is a relatively new concept.

In the late 1800s, advances and discoveries in history, sociology, archeology, and science were providing new windows into the world around us. Some scholars and theologians sought to reconcile all this new information with the ancient text in front of them. They engaged radical ideas like considering historical and cultural context, comparing manuscripts in original languages, or reviewing writing styles within books of the Bible. This challenged traditional ideas about authorship—for example, introducing ideas that several people wrote the Pentateuch instead of Moses or that the prophet Isaiah may have only written the first part of the book that bears his name. These new approaches all began to happen at this time, and some saw this as a threat to biblical inspiration and authority.[1]

This struggle with these areas of "higher criticism" is part of what spurred the fundamentalist-modernist controversy, which resulted in trials within some denominations for scholars who embraced new ideas.[2] It was then that others sought to erect boundaries around what we could believe about the Bible and how we ought to interpret it, and "inerrancy" as we know it was born. This theology asserted that (1) inspiration extends to the words of the Bible and not just the ideas, (2) Scripture teaches of its own inerrancy and inerrancy relates to any communicated fact whether physical, spiritual, doctrinal, philosophical, or psychological, and (3) inspiration and inerrancy apply primarily to the original autographs of Scripture. The validity of faith as they knew it hinged on there being no proven errors within the pages of Scripture.[3] Later on, this would result in denominational splits, and the group focused on inerrancy would be at the head of what became fundamentalism, which was the movement that birthed today's evangelicalism. But this theology tried to draw boxes where boundaries ought to be. It tried to simplify what is inherently complex and mysterious with a few key terms that we still have with us today.

Inerrancy

Inerrant, in short, means "without error." For those who hold inerrancy very tightly, this extends beyond the ideas of Scripture and into the details, even down to saying there are no copy errors in the original autographs (which we don't actually have and may never see). It means that every idea talked about in the Bible—physical, spiritual, doctrinal, philosophical, or psychological—is without any errors.[4]

That framework, however, does a bit of what it says not to do: it applies our modern categories to an ancient text. Reading the Bible this way can turn it into something it was never intended to be—a science textbook, unbiased historical record, or instruction manual. This is why concepts like evolution, gender, mental illness, or some historical data become contentious. We think the Bible must be accurate to be true, but it was not written with the intent to help us understand every academic discipline completely. Scholars like N. T. Wright, Scot McKnight, and Michael Bird showed me that Scripture has a different primary purpose—to tell us "the story of how the Creator is rescuing and restoring the whole creation, with his rescue and restoration of humans at the heart of it."[5]

Because the Bible was designed for that purpose, we can trust that it gives us all we need to know for salvation and life with God. In this way, I prefer the terms *infallible* and *sufficient* now over the ideas of the Bible being *inerrant* and *comprehensive.* They capture the essence of what inerrancy ought to mean: that the Bible is true in all it intends to affirm or teach. It is not a one-stop shop for accurate information on every subject in our world, but it does show us the way to God and the way to the world God is restoring.

Inspiration

Inspiration is the belief that the Holy Spirit had a role in the authoring of Scripture. This is widely accepted, but the extent to which the Holy Spirit directed the authors of the Bible is what is often up for debate. For the fundamentalists, the "verbal plenary inspiration" of the Scriptures is very important. This means that the very words chosen were specifically chosen by the Holy Spirit itself.[6] Some have even believed in a kind of mechanical inspiration in which the Holy Spirit overrode the faculties of the writer and just used him as a kind of device for recording exactly what the Spirit wanted to say.[7]

I grew up believing in the verbal plenary inspiration of the Bible—that every word was God's, every jot and tittle inspired directly. But as I started looking outside of the American evangelical influences I grew up with, scholars like Tim Mackie or Pete Enns, who've spent many years dedicated to studying the ancient contexts of the Bible, helped me see a variety of ways to take the Bible seriously as the words of God without it having to be exact.[8] Instead, we can tie it to God's intention as written through the authors (and sometimes arranged by editors) of the Bible's many books.[9] This frees us up to be attached to the patterns and ideas in the Bible without confining them to their original language, which is really what makes translations like the ones many of us have in our homes possible.

In the same way, the writers of the Bible were the translators of God's ideas to their people. It's why they use similar literary forms to the other cultures around them and images that made sense for their time and place.

Today, that's how I think of inspiration. Attaching the idea of inspiration to intention of message rather than its mechanics gives us freedom to move between contexts while remaining true to the written text that is doing its best to communicate the mysteries of God. The Holy Spirit gave the authors the ideas and concepts, and it was with those ideas that each author communicated in their own voice, experiences, and context. They weren't glorified transcriptionists or court reporters. They were artists of the written word given understanding that helps us to understand the things of God that are crucial to our salvation and life with God.[10] This is what makes the Bible sacred and authoritative.

Interpretation

What you believe about the above ideas can shape how you approach understanding what is written in the Bible and how it applies to you and everyone around you. If you believe the Bible to be inspired word-for-word by God and without any factual errors, then reading it literally becomes the prioritized approach to understanding it. The plain reading of Scripture, however, ends up being filtered through our context first, and that reading will then apply to any person or culture we encounter along the way. In a lot of ways, this elevates the interpretation of Scripture above the intent of Scripture, which makes any doctrinal disagreement a first-tier issue because it means the other side doesn't believe in the inerrancy or authority of the Bible.

When I started shifting some beliefs on issues like women in ministry in my evangelical circles, I started noticing inerrancy used this way as a defense of specific interpretations. Suddenly, if I didn't believe exactly what someone else believed about this issue, then I was outside the bounds of orthodoxy, a sinner in need of repentance for my low view of Scripture and the way of God. Inerrancy became the weapon of interpreters to keep questions at bay and everyone in uniform belief. It cut off conversations and closed doors. Have you ever experienced that? That you could believe 99 percent of the same things and find yourself on the outside because you had a different perspective on the final 1 percent?

I didn't ask questions because I thought *less* of the Bible. I asked *because* I still highly value Scripture. I adjusted my views because I believe the Bible is still relevant to me, because I believe that all truth is God's truth and the truth that exists outside the Bible does not have to be in conflict with the truth within its pages. I respect the Bible for what it is and what it intended to be—a complex library of books that tell the story of how a loving God interacts with humanity, renews all broken things, and invites me to participate.

Contextual Conversations

I was once in a discussion group led by Meredith Anne Miller, a pastor and children's ministry expert who helps parents tell Bible stories to their children.[11] As she talked about what the Bible was and wasn't and what to do about it, she told a story of a translator friend of hers who worked in a culture where they didn't have bread. So when Jesus says, "I am the bread of life," that wouldn't actually be helpful for them. Using that word would put up more barriers than lower them, which is the point of using the people group's language in the first place. Bread is sustenance in the Bible, and this people group had something that they consider a chief part of their sustenance—the sweet potato. In their Bible, Jesus is the sweet potato of life. It captures the intent without being more confusing to the reader, and it was made possible because the translators carefully applied the contexts of both the Bible and the present-day people group they were around.

If the story of Scripture is true—and I believe it is—then there must be sets of tools to translate its meaning for everyone on planet Earth, across time and space. For us, the challenge isn't so much the language we use—after all, we have many English translations of the Bible available to us at any moment—but the contexts we apply to find meaning and direction for our lives today. We need to be able to put the Bible into conversation with its various contexts so we can interpret well and apply what we see in Scripture to our lives in a way that transforms us and the world around us. In the rest of this chapter, I will unpack the contexts that have helped me the most in translating the Bible into my life.

Context 1: Story

Though the Bible is a complex library of literature, spanning centuries of time and many literary genres, it is also cohesive. There is one overarching narrative that connects the entire collection. The Bible builds on itself. It uses different authors (inspired by the same Holy Spirit) to tell one big story. This is called a meta-narrative. Understanding the story helps me understand the perspective I'm reading at any point within the Bible. It not only helps me unpack the mindset of the author, but it also helps me see the piece in light of the whole. Let's walk through the meta-narrative together.[12]

Creation

In the beginning, God created the world and humanity. Everything was good, and our relationship with and our status before God was unblemished. We were whole, integrated, thriving. There was order and peace.

Exile

Idolatry entered the picture when humankind chose to disobey God. This not only led to a disordering of each human's relationship with themselves and each other, but it also led to a disordering of relationship with God and the rest of creation. There were consequences of toil and strain placed upon us, and we were cast out of the uninhibited presence of God—exiled from our place of perfect peace.

Covenant

God had a plan, though. God would create order through a community of people chosen to be God's own, and they would choose to be a part of it just as they were chosen for it. This choice looked like a covenant commitment and the commitment would look like obedience to the Law that God established to help the community flourish. But the covenant was not one-sided. God, too, would keep a commitment. Through Abraham and Noah and Moses and David, God promised the Israelites they would have land of their own, many descendants, a king to bring victory, and the hope of the nations would come from them.

Redemption

But as it did with the humans at the beginning of the story, idolatry continued to show up; Israelites replaced the God who chose them with the priorities or deities of the neighboring communities. God's people would live through cycles of covenant renewal, peace, idolatry, and exile until Godself stepped physically, tangibly, completely into history in the person of Jesus Christ. Jesus, being fully God and fully man, would disrupt the cycle forever and make a way for full spiritual restoration and initiate the future completion of the physical restoration of the world.

Participation

Once again, a new community was established around this new reality that has begun through the work of Jesus. This community not only experienced the effects of spiritual restoration, but they modeled the physical restoration too. They became the bringers of heaven to earth—empowered by the Holy Spirit, partnering with the Father, living by the example and vision Jesus cast for them that would work for the full flourishing of all people.

Restoration

When the time is right, God will once again bring order from the chaos created by the sin and idolatry of humanity. Heaven and earth will be fully fused and restored, and Jesus will return to reign. Those who are a part of the new kingdom community will experience union with God without barriers and the world will be set right forever. Everything will be as it should be, just as it was in the beginning.

Without the whole story, parts of it feel hopeless or confusing (and I think they should feel that way sometimes), but with the whole story, we can see how those pieces fit in and how it shapes where the story is going. And we can also see something that looks one way up close in a completely new light when we zoom out to the big picture. Starting with the entire meta-narrative of Scripture gives us a compass for the long journey.

Context 2: Jesus as Word

My second semester of seminary I took a class in the church history department. I was very curious how the writers and leaders within the early church thought about church and Scripture and, well, everything. Over and over I noticed something in the readings my professor gave us—early church authors never used the term *word of God* to mean the Bible. They talked about Scripture at length, but only called it Scripture. It was a written revelation of God that they took seriously, but they reserved the term *the Word* for Jesus.[13] This also has to do with how the Greek word *logos* was used in that time. It often didn't just mean "word" like the ones I'm writing now to form sentences to communicate. It was an idea, a force behind creation and the world, a kind of completeness or perfection.[14] According to the gospel of John, Jesus is the embodiment of the Logos. He is the Word of God, and that means his life shows us God's postures and priorities so we can make them our own.

This felt like a lightbulb moment for me. The Bible is divine revelation; I believe that completely. But how much more important is the lived revelation that is contained in its pages? Jesus is the climax of God's story in the Bible. He was the linchpin of the plan—he brought redemption, gave rise to participation, and will reign in the restoration. He is the hope that was pointed to, the means of the promises contained in the Old Testament. That is the key differentiator of Christianity, which also makes him vital for the interpretation of Scripture.

I call this putting my Jesus goggles on. With these, I can look back to the Old Testament writings and see how they can be interpreted in light of Christ's lived revelation—not just in their own time (though doing that first is important) but how they might apply to mine. In the same way, we must look at all that Peter, Paul, John, and the other New Testament writers wrote through the lens of Jesus. It's like putting a photo filter over the Bible. It changes what you look for and what you see. What did Jesus preach and prioritize? What did the coming of Jesus mean for their salvation and for the world around them? What ought they to do because Jesus lived, died, and resurrected? The New Testament writers look at the world through the lived experience of Christ, and they would expect you to do the same. So I, too, have learned to put the Word of God at the center of the words of God. Those little bits that we pull from verses may look different when filtered through the life of Jesus.

Context 3: Literature

I am a book nerd. English was always my favorite subject in school—I love seeing all the ways creative people could put words together to form stories or ideas that captivated hearts and minds. I love seeing the threads of stories or thoughts come together in a climax. As a writer myself, I know that these do not often come together by accident. Instead, it takes planning and structure, and good writers also play with cultural expectations and references. Words, anecdotes, and more are carefully selected in reference to what the intended reader will understand. This is the art of storytelling, and a good writer will make use of these tools.

This is just as true for ancient literature, and even—maybe especially—the Bible. God used human authors to write this story, and each author's writing reflects both their voice and experience and what the Holy Spirit wanted them to communicate to God's people. The Bible tells God's story, and each author uses tools that help tell that story well, to a particular audience in a particular place as well as to all future readers across generations and continents. What I love about this is that it places the Bible in an established category with its own set of tools we can use to help us find meaning as we study: literature. So let's pretend we're back in English class for a moment and review the tools that help us understand a work of literature, and consider how they might help us read the Bible better.

Genre

What is the style of the book? We don't read a letter the same way we read a story, and the same goes for the variety of literature we find in the Bible. Within this anthology that tells God's story, we see narrative like in Genesis or Exodus, poetry like in Psalms, prophecy (which is often also poetic) like Isaiah, biographies like the gospels, and letters between familiars in the writings of Paul or Peter. Each of these genres is operating within certain structures or expected themes and images, and sometimes the authors even play with the genre by subverting the expectation either in structure or content—as in Paul's letter to the Galatians, where in the place the reader would traditionally expect encouragement, he expresses his anger, which sets the tone for what's to come. Knowing the genre helps us see how the author is communicating through the structure itself, and the genre can also help guide us in how straightforward we can be in our interpretations.[15]

Author

Who wrote it and why? Understanding an author can go a long way to helping us understand their writings. Take Paul, for example. He was a pragmatic, culturally conscious missionary. Understanding that helps us see that maybe his contradictions aren't contradictions at all. For example, his approach on women in churches seems to differ across his letters: Romans 16 where he commends many women who taught in or led churches, 1 Corinthians 11 where women may pray or prophesy like men can, 1 Corinthians 14 where women are to be silent, and 1 Timothy 2 where women are not to teach or have authority over men. Knowing Paul's approach, you might see that they're applications for different people and places. His agenda was to get the gospel everywhere, to let it take the shape that a particular culture needed it to—so he let it.

Audience

Who was this originally written to? The Bible is written *for* us, but it wasn't written *to* us at first. It becomes really easy to misread the text when we either don't fit or don't understand the original audience's mindset and culture. Knowing Matthew is primarily written to Jewish people and Luke to Greek people may help us understand why those authors chose certain themes, images, or stories to say important truths about Jesus, and it will certainly help us to better grasp what those important truths mean to us. An example of this is that Matthew quotes or alludes to the Old Testament the most of all the gospel writers. This is important for him because he is building a case for Christ as King or Messiah with familiar and important references for a Jewish audience.

Themes

One of the biggest lessons I learned in revisiting how I read the Bible was how often the big picture (the meta-narrative) and common themes inform what is happening in the specific book I'm reading. Not only should we always read on the lookout for the Bible's meta-narrative (or pieces of it), but we also must look at the key ideas and metaphors the author uses to communicate with the reader—creation, exodus, wilderness, kingdom or kingship, justice, or redemption are all examples of this. Often writers tie the sections of their book to the Bible's common themes, sometimes in way that bring more depth to stories you read or maybe change what individual words are meant to communicate. One example of this is the gospel of John's use of "in the beginning" and creation imagery in chapter 1 when communicating about Jesus as the Word and what that means for his divinity.

Structure and devices

What are the big ideas or arguments in the book? Here we take a look at the way the author builds their case for the point they are trying to make to their audience. When it's a gospel, you see why certain stories are there and why they may be in a certain order or next to other particular stories.

In the same way, an epistle is often structured to address certain issues facing a local church by making an argument pointing to their specific situation. The little parts add up to the big parts, so when we take the littler parts out of their bigger context, we may change the meaning.

Sentences and words

How does the author phrase what they're trying to say and why? This is the part that I learned to focus on when I was in Sunday school and youth group (and even my first time in seminary). We spent our time drilling down line by line, but this is actually a last step for me now. When we have done the higher-level literary work, we have a more focused lens through which to view the details. Words may take on new meanings, or we may need to look up some words to see why they would be used here and in this way. We can diagram sentences and parse words, but we must do so in light of the big ideas that surround them. It's why we can know what "light" literally means, but also recognize that different authors will use the term differently. For example, in John, Jesus as the light is a prevailing metaphor throughout the book, but in Matthew, it's used in a variety of ways to talk about the effects of the message of Jesus or the work of his followers. The context changes the meaning of the word, and it is important to respect each usage within each context.

When we look at the Bible as a collection of literature, we can see not only how it builds on itself but also what it wants us to know about God and the people in the stories. Knowing this extra bit of context has proven to be the best tool I've found for understanding the Bible. And even better, this is not something that requires years of study to figure out. Most study Bibles and lots of free online tools are available to find most of this information quickly and concisely.[16]

Context 4: Community

You may have heard the ideas above at different times throughout your life. As a very good evangelical, I learned all the inductive Bible study methods, and I could break down a sentence or verse with the best of them. But one practice has truly shaped my approach to Scripture like no other: reading it in community.

When you read through Scripture, there are a lot of "you shall" or "you shall not" phrases. The thing you may not see, because English is weird, is that a whole lot of those are actually a plural *you*, a *y'all*, if you will indulge the Texan in me for a moment.[17] The Hebrew Bible was written mostly for the community of Israel. The Pentateuch was their law and origin story. The psalms were their hymnal. The prophets and history books were their historical record, and the wisdom books were guides to help them live, well, wisely. And they were written for this community.

In the same way, the New Testament books, with few exceptions (I'm looking at you, Philemon and Timothy), were written to entire communities. The gospels had wide audiences in mind, and most of Paul's letters were written to specific church communities. We miss something when we don't engage Scripture outside of our own private devotional time or while consuming it from the pew. It was meant for all of us to work out meaning together.

This was a common Jewish practice too. Rabbis and groups of Jewish people would read Scripture and discuss meanings together in their Midrash tradition, which can take the form of debate or commentary writing.[18] The idea of personal Bible study is very new and actually a very big privilege! Having a printed Bible in the home, let alone one of your own (or more if you're like me) is a luxury—not just back then but even now in some places in the world. Reading Scripture in groups is the norm when access to a personal or family Bible is not available, as was the case for most of Christian history. Though time and technology have given many of us access to the personal Bible in a variety of ways, reading Scripture in community is still beneficial to our understanding. This communal approach can be engaged in two ways: tradition and together.

Tradition

We have spent a lot of time understanding how to read the Bible as history and literature, but it's more than that. It is also theology—it communicates to us truths about the God of Israel who graciously extended welcoming arms to include us all. (The word *theology* literally means the study of God.) The believers who came before us pulled together these time-less truths on which we all stand into creeds and hymns, which we speak and sing aloud. These truths then help us read Scripture through their eyes, seeing what they saw for ourselves. This connects us across time to believers through-out the ages and creates a community of thought that can help shape how we think about what we read in the words of Scripture.

Together

The next way we engage Scripture in community is by read-ing and discussing it with others. Each of us has limited experience, expertise, exposure to ideas, resources, and education. But together, we have something important to share and something important to learn. Everyone may see a different detail that brings Scripture to life again for you. One of my friends is incredible at putting herself in the emotional shoes of the people we read about. Another has a robust background in history, and he brings such good information about the societies we read about in the Bible. I learn so much from my friends because they have so much knowledge, perspective, and experience that I don't. Like all works of literature, there are many layers to consider. Because of my limited knowledge or experience, I tend to see only a few of the possible layers or interpretations. Bringing others to the table with diverse viewpoints and experiences exposes me to new ideas and maybe puts me in a different place in the passage.

I recently heard an example of a man who taught on the dry bones in Ezekiel 37 in seminary preaching class. He spoke as though he was the prophet, but his professor said that in his tradition, they would be more likely to read it as though they were the dry bones.[19] That new perspective can shift how we think about the stories we read and the lesson we learn, and through discussion we can find our minds and our hearts changed. Doing this in person is great, but you can also get these perspectives by reading widely from a variety of backgrounds and viewpoints. You don't have to know someone personally in order to learn from them.

We are all united to Christ and empowered with the Holy Spirit, and together with the community of saints that has gone before us, we find our guardrails and our path forward through Scripture much more powerfully than we ever could alone. It is together that we are transformed.

One More Thing

It is all well and good to learn to read Scripture better and put
it in conversation with its many contexts to plumb the depth
of its riches. But if I could leave you with one key insight, it
would be this: You are not a second-class reader of the Bible.
The Holy Spirit who lives in the pastors and teachers who
have influenced you is the same Holy Spirit who lives in you.
Training is great, but few churches and households and followers of Jesus across the world have training. Even fewer
have been to seminary, and many don't even know what a
seminary is! So even though I have shared these tools that
help me have a conversation with the Bible, I want you to
know that you—just as you are right now—are capable of getting what is needed from the Bible because the Holy Spirit
is in you. With a little humility, a few good questions, and a
whole lotta help from the Spirit and our friends, we can see
what God has for us.

As I wrestled with my new and very foreign experiences,
I realized that I had been given specific rules for engagement
with the Bible that I wasn't sure worked anymore. I hadn't
been taking the Bible on its own terms but on mine. When
I stripped away my previous assumptions and began to look
for God more than myself in the pages of Scripture, I realized
that there remained some dissonance between what I was
taught and what I found there. Learning to use new tools and
lenses for the Bible helped me to better translate what I read
into more timeless principles that made sense of my experiences with others in different nations and cultures.

But more than that, it showed me God's character and
God's priorities. My cultural priorities were not the same as
God's priorities and some of my beliefs were challenged and

changed. I learned that the greatest tool for my deconstruction—past, present, and future—is the Bible itself. It didn't happen in spite of the Bible but because of it. And in the rest of these pages, you'll see some of the tangles I had in my faith and the truths I found in Scripture that led me to a more joyful, hopeful, and loving faith.

THREE

The Whole Gospel

"THIS CHURCH IS everything to me," he said, his eyes glistening with tears.

Dhonu's family had left him for dead. He had been sick for a long time, and they couldn't afford his medicine or care. He was a burden they could no longer bear. As his body wasted away from his illness, they made the decision to leave him to his end and walk away. They drove up the mountainside and left him there.

But as though emerging straight out of the parable of the Good Samaritan, someone from a local church found Dhonu on the mountainside. Without thinking, they ran to help him. They carried him to the church, cleaned him up, and gave him a place to rest. That week the church members gave their money to purchase the medicine he needed to be healed, and over time, he was.

When I met Dhonu, it was months later, in that little thatched roof church in the mountains of South Asia. It wasn't just his church, it was his home. It was, in his words, everything. He found care . . . he found a family . . . and he also found Jesus. This brief encounter changed so much about how I thought about our mission as a church.

For that church, there weren't two separate missions: caring for souls or caring for bodies. Nope. For them these two missions were tied together deeply, and their care for Dhonu was the embodied example. After sitting with Dhonu and the members of the church there, we drove down the mountain to the hotel for the night. I stared quietly out the window, watching the fog from my breath appear then disappear over and over. I pondered what it would mean to be the kind of church that called people back to life both physically and spiritually.

For a long time, I believed that spiritual needs were most important. I think I might still believe that, but what I've also learned is that those needs are often wrapped in layers upon layers of other needs that must be tended to: physical, emotional, relational. We are humans having a human experience. That requires a body and a soul, and sometimes you can't even get to a spiritual need without first working through the physical ones. And maybe the problem is that we try to compartmentalize these parts of ourselves to begin with. But back then, the mission was purely spiritual. We could knock on apartment doors and evangelize but forget to ask how we could help otherwise. The value of the interaction hinged on the state of the occupant's soul before and after. For us and for many Christians, saving souls rose above caring for bodies. After all, our flesh is corrupt and we only need our souls to get to heaven, right? Dhonu and that tiny church in South Asia showed me how doing that was not just missing opportunities, but maybe also missing the point.

What if God cares for bodies as much as God cares for souls? What if God doesn't just want to redeem the spiritual part of us but every part of us? What if the Christian life isn't about compartmentalizing ourselves but pursuing wholeness?

The Whole Gospel for the Whole World

Stunned and sad, I watched an endless stream of cable news in the summer of 2020. I couldn't stop because I wanted it all to make sense. More than anything, I wondered how there could be such varied responses to the events taking over my social media news feeds. The tension had been building in the United States for a few years, but that summer we reached a boiling point that erupted in protests against racism and police brutality after yet another killing of a Black person.

- Eric Garner (July 17, 2014)

- Michael Brown (August 9, 2014)

- Laquan McDonald (October 20, 2014)

- Tamir Rice (November 22, 2014)

- Walter Scott (April 4, 2015)

- Samuel DuBose (July 19, 2015)

- Freddie Gray (April 12, 2015)

- Alton Sterling (July 5, 2016)

- Philando Castile (July 6, 2016)

- Ahmaud Arbery (February 23, 2020)

- Breonna Taylor (March 13, 2020)

- George Floyd (May 25, 2020)[1]

After writing out that list, I find I have to pause and take a deep breath. Those names, now recognized in households across the US, each represent a Black man or woman whose life was taken from them; most of these deaths occurred at the hands of or while in the custody of police officers. Reading them still brings on a wave of deep grief, along with frustration that I know only this handful of names of Black men and women who've lost their lives at the hands of those meant to protect us—all of us, and this list doesn't even include those who have been victims of violence since George Floyd. The summer of 2020 felt like a moment we should have been ready for as Christians. Repentance is part of our regular practice, and this seemed like the time to call for it. It was our time to weep with those who wept, to be grieved at the loss of life, and to care for those who were suffering.

#BlackLivesMatter became the cry on so many lips as people stood up to demand attention and justice for the lives lost and for the many others harmed due to centuries of prejudice, discrimination, and injustice. To me, it seemed like a no-brainer to talk about this injustice, to call for justice, and to do what I could to work for justice too. The church is charged with this very work—to "do justice" (Micah 6:8)— and yet in that critical moment we largely fell short.

I was struck by the responses that I received from believers I knew. "It's not a skin problem. It's a sin problem," "All lives matter," and the one I understood the least, "Just preach the gospel," were repeated so often I think people must have just been copying and pasting them everywhere anyone mentioned racism. I was confused by the disconnect then, and I continue to be confused by it now. Faced with the same reality, my friends and I had a very different reaction. We kept coming back to a few simple questions, like "Why was it so hard to believe that sinful humans get it wrong, sometimes in egregious ways?" and "Why can't we be supportive of authority *and* call for accountability?" We were frustrated at having to choose sides that didn't make sense, that somehow keeping our allegiance to our spiritual priorities might lead to excusing, condoning, or even committing violence against the physical bodies that contain those souls.

It was the same disconnect I felt when we were driving down the mountain in South Asia. My gospel had become too small. I had connected the work of the gospel to the work of the spiritual alone in my mind, and social justice—the work of righting wrongs and creating equity on earth by actively serving and meeting needs individually and corporately— had somehow became a dirty word. I was now beginning to see that this gospel was incomplete. If we're looking at Jesus' life, we see that this kind of care isn't opposed to the gospel. It's actually part of our gospel work.

The Holistic Ministry of Jesus

I learned more about this kind of gospel work from my friend Beka, who shared with me a powerful story of an experience she had on a mission trip to South Asia. Part of my job back then was to sit with those who went on trips to hear some of their stories and what they learned so I could share it with others. The trips in this particular place were very focused on evangelism, but they didn't count out other ways of ministering to the people they encountered on the field. One day Beka came to the home of a woman with an ailment. After listening to the woman, the translator suggested that Beka pray for her healing. Beka was nervous.

She asked her translator, "What if God doesn't do it? What if he doesn't want her whole?"

He responded, "Of course he wants her whole. Maybe not on earth, but then in heaven. We can pray for that now because we know some day she can suffer no more."

I think about that story often. Of course, neither the translator nor Beka thought the women wasn't a whole person just as she was. The challenge was to believe that God wants to remove the pain and suffering we experience in our physical bodies as much as in our spiritual selves. God wants our spiritual healing—believing that seems to be the easy part—but God also wants our physical wholeness, relieving us from pain and suffering (Revelation 21:4–5). Whether in this life or in eternity, we will be restored fully, and though that may not mean we will all have what society considers a perfect body—because all shapes, sizes, and scars are welcome in eternity—we can pray for healing today, and we can claim the promise that healing and wholeness are God's desire for us.

This idea changed so much about how I thought about ministry, and it applies to all of us believers who are out here doing the work of God. If God wants our bodies and souls to be complete, then part of bringing God's kingdom "on earth as it is in heaven" means partnering with God to be agents of that completion. Physical care is part of our spiritual ministry, because humans aren't just souls. We are souls in a physical body. Our work must be holistic because people's needs are holistic. When we care for holistic needs, we find ourselves with more opportunities to affect lives spiritually because we have done the work of building relationships and credibility while demonstrating the love of Jesus in a tangible way. In my own experience, when I am in survival mode, I can think of little else than meeting the need I have in the moment, and it is only when the stress of those days is behind me that I can think about higher needs, and I trust the people who were with me along the way to help me work through them.

The gospel can be experienced before it is heard, and the door for evangelism swings wide open when people know you see them and care for them. This creates opportunity for true wholeness and flourishing. When we divorce holiness from wholeness, we miss the big idea. Holiness is the goal because wholeness is the point. Holiness allows us to draw near to God in order to be whole, no longer separating the parts of us that are heavenly and the parts of us that are earthly. This goes beyond ourselves and into our communities and even the world, helping all to flourish in our wholeness. The full gospel is the "whole" gospel.

Jesus modeled this for us clearly in the gospels. His ministry was a blend of healing, exorcism, and preaching. Take a look at this short section from Mark 1 when Jesus began his ministry:

> They went to Capernaum, and when the Sabbath came, he entered the synagogue and taught. They were astounded at his teaching, for he taught them as one having authority and not as the scribes. Just then there was in their synagogue a man with an unclean spirit, and he cried out, "What have you to do with us, Jesus of Nazareth? Have

you come to destroy us? I know who you are, the Holy One of God."

But Jesus rebuked him, saying, "Be quiet and come out of him!" And the unclean spirit, convulsing him and crying with a loud voice, came out of him. They were all amazed, and they kept on asking one another, "What is this? A new teaching—with authority! He commands even the unclean spirits, and they obey him." At once his fame began to spread throughout the surrounding region of Galilee.

As soon as they left the synagogue, they entered the house of Simon and Andrew, with James and John. Now Simon's mother-in-law was in bed with a fever, and they told him about her at once. He came and took her by the hand and lifted her up. Then the fever left her, and she began to serve them. (Mark 1:21–31)

In this segment alone, Jesus preaches in a synagogue, casts out demons, and heals Simon's mother-in-law. In the rest of the chapter he goes on to heal the sick and possessed in the crowd that surrounded Simon's mother-in-law's home, preached in Galilee, and cleansed a leper. These were not separate parts of his work. He didn't tell the sick and demon-possessed that all they needed was the gospel. Instead he took care of the whole persons in front of him. The healing, exorcism, and preaching were all part of the work. In Mark 7–8, Jesus heads into lands occupied primarily by Gentiles, where he exorcises a demon from afar, heals a deaf man, then preaches to the multitude before he feeds them. In that sequence, the healing and exorcisms came first. Before he preached to bring people to wholeness spiritually, he sought to make them whole physically. Even after it all, he cared for their physical bodies by meeting the most basic of needs: food.

Jesus didn't take this on as only his mission either. In Mark 6, he sends out the twelve disciples with similar tasks.

> He called the twelve and began to send them out two by two and gave them authority over the unclean spirits. . . . So they went out and proclaimed that all should repent. They cast out many demons and anointed with oil many who were sick and cured them. (Mark 6:7, 12–13)

We often think of our gospel work in terms of the great commission (Matthew 28:16–20): preaching, baptizing, and teaching. But if Jesus' life is the epitome of gospel work then we should take seriously the physical implications of gospel work, too. I think that begins with seeing the gospel story for what it truly is . . . a justice story.

The Holistic Gospel

Did you know there are actually four types of justice? According to *Sociology Guide*, these four types are distributive, procedural, retributive, and restorative.

- *Distributive justice* cares about creating economic equality in order to give everyone in society a fair share of benefits and resources.

- *Procedural justice* is about ensuring all the proper processes are followed in a justice system in order to protect the chances of unbiased decisions.

- *Retributive justice* punishes an offender for their wrongdoing or past injustice.

- *Restorative justice,* however, "focuses on violations as crimes against individuals. It is concerned with healing victims' wounds, restoring offenders to law-abiding lives, and repairing harm done to interpersonal relationships and the community."[2]

Growing up in evangelical circles, I was most often taught to think of justice in terms of retributive justice, even in the gospel story. Taking into consideration the meta-narrative, as we discussed in the last chapter, the overarching biblical story arc is one of restorative justice. When we look through that lens, we will also find that every dimension of justice is present in various ways throughout the Bible. Let's unpack how justice—in its fullness—shapes our lives and gospel work now, and in another chapter we will dive deeper into how it shapes our full and future restoration.

But before we move into the justice aspect of the gospel, we need to define the gospel. When I talk about the gospel, I mean the redemptive story of humanity that begins in Eden, where Adam and Eve were made to have fellowship with God, but colossally messed that up. Jesus came to make it right. He took what we messed up, and he bore it on the cross. He hit the big reset button for our relationship with God by taking away the sins and mess-ups that keep us from God. Now we are active partners in how God is restoring humanity and the earth for eternity, taking on the mantle to care for creation that we were given in the garden. The gospel is the basis of our salvation. We receive this salvation by believing this story, repenting from our sins, and accepting the forgiveness of God now available to us through Christ's sacrifice.

Now, what does this have to do with justice? Well, the breaking of our relationship with God happened as a consequence of sin and disobedience to God. I often find myself looking back in disdain at Adam and Eve thinking, "You had *one* job." But though I might entertain the idea that I would do it better, it doesn't change the reality that we were affected by their mistake. As time went on, the Law and then Jesus revealed to us what God expected of God's people, and every time we don't meet that standard, we sin. Our sin carries consequences as it did for Adam and Eve. Justice meant that we wouldn't be able to be with God again, not in Adam and Eve's original state of intimacy and certainly not for eternity.

Punishment and offerings were typical ways to remediate these rifts in the Old Testament, but at least in the gospel I grew up with, God paid the price through Jesus (retributive justice). He was our substitute who willingly served our time and made it possible to wipe our slates clean.[3] This is called *justification*—the removal of our guilt and reinstatement of our righteousness. Acceptance, confession, and repentance pave our way back to God (procedural justice).

Yet God didn't just reconcile us spiritually. Our God is a God of wholeness. The story doesn't stop with the atoning death of Christ for our sins. You know what God does next? It's wild, but it's true. God resurrects Jesus in his physical body. It's not magic; it's miraculous. This act makes it possible for us to be restored to our original state in the garden, when we were deemed "very good." We were humans who had been shaped by God's hands and breathed to life by breath from Godself, and because of Jesus, when we move toward God, we begin our journey back to that state. The spiritual is now restored, and the promise of the restoration of the physical body awaits us all. The hope of resurrection is alive in us all now. There is now victory for us and for all creation.

Wholeness isn't just for our souls. It's for every part of us.

The Holistic Call to Reconciliation

So how does having our righteousness restored relate to restorative justice for our communities? I learned something about the concept of righteousness in my first semester of Greek that unlocked this connection for me. The word we often translate as *righteousness* in the New Testament (*dikaiosune*) can also be translated as *justice*.[4] In fact, when I shared this on Twitter, people who spoke other languages told me their language's word for *justice* is often used interchangeably with *righteousness*, like in Spanish, or has the same root word, like in Ukrainian.[5] This isn't just a New Testament Greek phenomenon, either. In the Old Testament, though there are distinct words for righteousness and justice, we often see them paired as synonyms or parallel ideas for emphasis, especially in Psalms, Proverbs, and the Prophets. When we see that God has made us righteous because of our salvation through the gospel, what we really see is that God's justice is served on our behalf and is restored through Christ.

It may seem like a small quibble to try to parse the difference between the two words if they do mean the same thing, but for many of us they've actually come to mean different things. We think of righteousness as our personal standing before God, and justice as more communal because it involves making things right between at least two parties or observing mutually accepted guidelines for order and morality. When I first learned that in the Bible the two words could be the same or at least often went together, I found myself facing another question: How much of our lives, our culture, our faith would be different if we saw righteousness not in personal terms, but rather as a communal pursuit of justice?

- What if it's not a "breastplate of righteousness" that we wear but a "breastplate of justice" (Ephesians 6:14)?

- What if we pursued justice, godliness, faith, love, and endurance instead of personal righteousness first on the list (1 Timothy 6:11)?

- What if the judges mentioned in Hebrews 11:32–34 were commended for administering justice (NRSVue) versus performing acts of personal righteousness (NASB)?

- What if we're to be quick to listen, slow to speak, and slow to anger so we produce God's justice versus personal righteousness (James 1:19–20)?

This idea sparks an endless stream of questions, but chief among them is: Would we feel different about the word *justice* if we saw it this way?

Justice holds us together, and justice can also heal us. That's why I find restorative justice to be a helpful construct here, because it doesn't just describe what God did for us. It also shows us what we're to do now that we've received and benefited from it. If we go back to the great commission, we see that we are saved in order to participate in the work of the gospel to transform lives and make disciples, and the work of the gospel is both spiritual and physical restoration. We are reconciled and entrusted with sharing this reconciliation with others. Here's how Paul puts it in 2 Corinthians 5:17–21:

So if anyone is in Christ, there is a new creation: everything old has passed away; look, new things have come into being! All this is from God, who reconciled us to himself through Christ and has given us the ministry of reconciliation; that is, in Christ God was reconciling the world to himself, not counting their trespasses against them, and entrusting the message of reconciliation to us. So we are ambassadors for Christ, since God is making his appeal through us; we entreat you on behalf of Christ: be reconciled to God. For our sake God made the one who knew no sin to be sin, so that in him we might become the righteousness of God.

We are now righteous *and* entrusted with the message and ministry of spiritual justice, and through the Holy Spirit's presence we are prompted to do God's work in the world. God's priorities have always included ritual spiritual dimensions as well as the relationships and well-being of communities. A stroll through the Law given to Moses shows us that God cared about how people took care of one another by leaving extra wheat harvested in the fields for the poor (Leviticus 23, Deuteronomy 24), how they paid each other for harm done by animals or people (Exodus 22), and how they made space for the foreigners to be a part of their community (Leviticus 19, Deuteronomy 10 and 27) (distributive justice). Even in the New Testament, James writes, "Religion that is pure and undefiled before God the Father is this: to care for orphans and widows in their distress and to keep oneself unstained by the world" (James 1:27). The intersection of faith and justice has always been alive, and we are the ones who have been empowered to bring God's whole justice to the whole world.

We cannot compartmentalize the work. When we take on only the spiritual mantle and not the physical one, we miss opportunities for both, and they belong together. I once heard pastor Tony Evans say in a sermon, "Righteousness and justice are twin towers."[6] Two sides, one coin. The gospel does more than save us from judgment. It saves us for justice.

Choosing Justice

Grasping this idea of the "whole" gospel made me love the gospel even more. Finally, I had a story that wasn't just good news for eternity but good news for today, and not just for the privileged but for the poor and oppressed that I met at home and overseas. It didn't just mean redemption would be complete someday, but that it was coming through us to the world too.

I'll admit that this idea holds a lot of tension for me and the circles I inhabit. Because of sin and its consequences, the way we interact with each other and the world has been tainted. It's through the work of the Holy Spirit that we are empowered to change this on every level, and this begins when the Spirit indwells us at salvation. But today, much of the tension in this area exists because of how different believers answer these two questions:

1. Which ought to be the priority—physical or spiritual?

2. What is the best way to express our faith in the public square?

The first question presents a real challenge, because we know that spiritually the world's needs are great, and they are unchangeable outside of Christ. And if you believe in an afterlife with consequences—regardless of the specifics related to their form and duration, then there are more than earthly consequences to our spiritual paths. On the other hand, we know that people are dying every day of real disease, pain, and suffering. What does it tell them about God to care little for their bodies? Can we even hope to help people spiritually if we ignore their physical need? Both are to be part of our work, and how we meet those needs will depend heavily on the situation and the leading of the Spirit.

So how do we approach the second question? Ultimately, it's a matter of how we wish to express our values. How do we show we're different from the world? Do we preach? Do we give? What do we do? There isn't one answer. There is no dichotomy here, no either/or solution. It's a "yes, and" situation. We show our love in word and deed. We embrace the tension because our world needs both, and the way of the kingdom requires both too. We don't do this *for* our salvation but *because* of it. They aren't contradictory but complementary.

Later in the gospel of Mark, we see Jesus in the temple in Jerusalem facing questions from all kinds of religious authorities. A scribe approaches him and asks a pressing question: What's the most important commandment?

Jesus answered, "The first is, 'Hear, O Israel: the Lord our God, the Lord is one; you shall love the Lord your God with all your heart and with all your soul and with all your mind and with all your strength.' The second is this, 'You shall love your neighbor as yourself.' There is no other commandment greater than these." Then the scribe said to him, "You are right, Teacher; you have truly said that 'he is one, and besides him there is no other'; and 'to love him with all the heart and with all the understanding and with all the strength' and 'to love one's neighbor as one-self'—this is much more important than all whole burnt offerings and sacrifices." (Mark 12:29–33)

Our faith in Jesus and empowerment in the Holy Spirit are what enable us to break through the barrier that keeps heaven and earth from coming together. It now comes together in us and through us. Loving God and loving our neighbor are demonstrations of how the spiritual and physical are of chief importance to God, which means carrying the spiritual and physical justice to every part of the world we possibly can.

There may be tension, but there is no choice to be made between doing justice and preaching the gospel or loving God and loving others. It's our job to work to do both because Jesus did both, to fight the narrative that to do one is to reject or lower the importance of the other, to allow the Spirit and our relationships to guide us in leaning into whichever side needs to win out in each moment. Both bring glory to God and life to those around us. Loving our neighbor *is* loving God.

I was once part of a group that was laser-focused on sharing the gospel with people we met throughout the week—grocery store clerks, baristas, people in our group fitness class at the gym, or the person we happened to sit next to on public transporta-tion. I meant well back then, but to see everyone as a potential target for your message is also to feel the pressure of not doing enough. What if they never heard the good news because I was answering an important email or call on my phone and missed my one opportunity to connect? There was something freeing about realizing that anything I do for another is part of sharing the gospel. I bought a friend groceries when they needed some-thing off their plate after a major surgery and helped another pay a bill for a prescription that they couldn't afford. My husband helped someone he knew fix his car to make it to all the appointments they had between work, health, and home life, and he talked another friend through figuring out their financial needs so they can make decisions about the best job to be secure and healthy at the same time. Each of these are ways we showed love to those in our lives by supporting their wholeness. Watching them find their way to flourishing in any part of their lives is part of the joyful work of the kingdom.

Beyond that, it was a relief to my own self that God cared about what was happening to me physically in my body. I used to feel ashamed for thinking about my sickness or being preoccupied with my suffering, because I still had good news for my soul. One year I spent at least six months straight sick in some way. I had an ulcer that disrupted my life, migraines that didn't stop, and some kind of rash that broke out on my back. In all that, I thought I just had to trudge on and remain grateful that the important parts of my life—the spiritual ones—were taken care of. My soul was good, but my body felt broken. I didn't really know if God cared about that, but the ministry of Jesus showed me that God does care about that pain and the suffering that comes out of it like new limitations and alienation from community. I find it easier now to take care of my body, knowing that how I care for and use this physical vessel is part of my worship and work for God.

There is no compartmentalizing. The physical and the spiritual exist in each of us, and they exist in Jesus, the one who made the restoration of both possible. We neither *have* to choose nor *get* to choose one over the other. The whole world needs the whole gospel, and there is freedom to be found when we offer it to ourselves and to others.

FOUR

A More Tangible Hope

I PULLED MY scarf up over my nose and mouth because the smoke was starting to choke me a little. We were standing across the river from the fire, but the gentle valley wind was blowing it our direction along with the wailing of a grieving mother. We had found ourselves in a Hindu temple on the other side of the world where ritual cremation took place. This was one of the most holy ways to part with the body of a loved one if you were Hindu in this country—this river, this ritual. Ironically, the person being cremated that day in South Asia had been in a car accident near his college in Texas, which just happened to be less than a mile from the place I lived at the time. He had been overseas for school, and his family flew his body home to be handled with care. Wrapped carefully and covered with flowers and colored powder, traditional to the culture and religion, his family walked his body to the pyre to find rest forever in the river.

I had always found burial to be a very strange ritual as a young person, and as I grew into an adult, I figured I'd just be cremated. Why spend the money and the land just to have my body decompose? Back then, I didn't think it mattered what happened to my body because it's just going to go away. Bodies aren't needed in heaven, and that's where I was going. My soul would end up where it needed to be, and that's all that mattered, right? But that's not how many have seen it in the history of the church, or even in its present.

Walking through the cathedrals and abbeys of England, you will find monuments and burial sites of kings, queens, and notable figures in the country's history. You will find more in the smaller churches that dot the countryside, like Holy Trinity Church in Stratford-upon-Avon where Shakespeare lies. He actually has prime real estate in the chancel, which is the part of an Anglican church where the clergy and choir may be, near the altar. But my favorite burial places are the ones that surround the tiny village churches. To walk up to these churches' doors, you often must walk through a cemetery. The grass is tall and headstones in varying shades of gray peek out of it, each one with the name of the faithful ones who lie beneath inscribed to honor them. Generally trying to face east, they look forward to the new day dawning where they will experience physical resurrection. This is the hope they have—a fully embodied life in the future.

Finding the False Narrative

The future that was most celebrated in my early Christian life was not very earthy or embodied. Quite the opposite, actually. In the evangelical churches I grew up in, our main hope was heaven. We looked forward to either death or to the end of all things where we would escape the dreadful earth we were attached to, and our souls would glide up to the heavenly worship party. We saw the new Jerusalem that Revelation was going on about as a kind of satellite city in the sky, where all our souls would gather together after earth was gone. In these same spaces, there was also a heavy focus on the "end times." The pastors and teachers saw Revelation as a roadmap for understanding our current landscape as they led us to the end of days—finding a "mark of the beast" in every popular tattoo design and the antichrist in every charismatic world leader.

Books and movies like *Left Behind* were part of the popular culture, and I found myself with such intense rapture anxiety that I actually couldn't bring myself to read Revelation until I was in my late twenties. I simply took teachers' word for it because I couldn't bear to look at the monsters and mayhem that awaited the future in case I was left behind. But as I traveled and wrote about the goal of the mission of God and how it brought together every nation, tribe, tongue, and people (Revelation 7:9), I began to suspect that Revelation wasn't quite as scary as I had been told. Once I started reading it for myself, I realized that no one told me the end of the story! And the end of the story changed *everything* about how I view our final hope today.

Whether intentionally or not, those who influenced my early Christian education favored the spiritual over the physical—not just in their idea of salvation, as we discussed in the last chapter, but also in their idea of the eternal dwelling of God's people. The goal was to leave behind your body so you wouldn't be left behind in the part of the world that would be destroyed. Souls mattered, but bodies were corrupted and would be done away with.

This kind of thinking tips into gnosticism—a heresy from the early days of the church. In those gnostic teachings, there was a strong duality between physical and spiritual, and the end goal of all history was for the physical to dissolve and everyone to return to their purely spiritual state. This had ramifications for how people pursued God. The simple version of the process born from this theology was that (a) you can achieve perfection through a special and exclusive revelation about God that only a few had, (b) this secret knowledge was more important than any other belief or practice, and (c) when you reach the right level of knowledge and experience with the divine, you would transcend the physical and become a completely spiritual being without any of the physical matter that was considered corrupt.[1] This made gnostics a kind of elite group because they didn't focus on worldly matters, and the knowledge they kept would only be given to a few. It also made the main problem of humanity its physicality rather than sin and guilt, and the groups of those who held this theology also rejected some of the traditions and rituals of the church—like the sacraments. In the end, gnosticism was deemed a heresy because of these issues,[2] but the mindset didn't disappear after that declaration.

Following from this line of thinking, I was also taught that our world was caught in an inevitable downward spiral into chaos and immorality. We could really do nothing about it, and only the return of Christ to reign in the end would create order and perfection again. The decay of the earth and the crumbling of society, by our measures, was merely a sign of the times. Soon Jesus would come back, and then he would sweep us into his arms and up to heaven while the earth below us would be destroyed. We would finally be right where we belonged, in the safety and spiritual perfection of heaven.

These ideas also fueled our urgency in missions. We needed to save souls because Christ would be coming back very soon. That goal had to be the top priority to the exclusion of many other physically focused ministries. Escaping to heaven also meant escaping our physical forms and living in the spiritual, and purer, realm of God. Can you see how this tips into a kind of functional gnosticism? Were there ways the theology and action you grew up with showed these same tendencies? And if so, how was this displayed in the priorities of preaching or programs in your church?

But now, I believe the Bible tells a different story from that narrative I grew up with. To understand the end, we must actually go back to the beginning. Because here's the thing about stories: the end is often a lot like the beginning. Order has been restored once the conflict that kicked the story into gear has been resolved. This is why we enjoy sitcoms. Everyone ends up right where they started at the end of the episode. It gives us a sense of equilibrium and continuity. In the same way, the end of the Bible is much like its beginning. But if we don't start where our story starts, we might not quite make sense of what we see in its final pages. So like a good novel reader, I will start there. And in this one, the hope in the story is integrated, embodied, and actually pretty earthly after all.

In the Beginning

Have you ever heard the term *thin places*? It's an idea that gained popularity in Celtic tradition. A thin place describes a location where the barrier between heaven and earth is thin—where the two mingle and intertwine, and one can be on earth but also close to the divine.[3] The plan God had for God's people was one of sacred spaces, a whole world of thin places where humanity and God meet without barriers, a place where the physical and spiritual are fused together in harmony. You see it right from the start:

> Then God said, "Let us make humans in our image, according to our likeness, and let them have dominion over the fish of the sea and over the birds of the air and over the cattle and over all the wild animals of the earth and over every creeping thing that creeps upon the earth." So God created humans in his image, in the image of God he created them; male and female he created them. (Genesis 1:26–27)

> Then the Lord God formed man from the dust of the ground and breathed into his nostrils the breath of life, and the man became a living being. And the Lord God planted a garden in Eden, in the east, and there he put the man whom he had formed. (Genesis 2:7–8)

The garden of Eden was our first sacred space. God's relationship with humans was intimate from the beginning. No other creatures were made in God's own image or to have God's breath in their being. This made us more than physical beings—it made us spiritual. And this gave us the capacity to fellowship with God in a way that no other creature could.

For creatures like that—the "very good" kind—God did something that continues to surprise me: God planted a

=2l

garden and placed humans there. Adam and Eve were there to work the land, watch over it, and walk with God. And it's in the garden that they met with God unimpeded by rituals and barriers. It was a place where God dwells . . . where heaven and earth mix seamlessly and where everything is just right. There's a word for this kind of place and state of being: *shalom*.

For a while I lived in an area of Dallas that has a large Jewish population. It was not unusual to see Jewish people running into each other in public and greeting each other with the customary "Shalom." This word is often translated as *peace*, which makes it a lovely sentiment to offer someone as you pass by. Like many Hebrew words, this one is deeper, wider, and more complex. It's much more than a platitude of peace. Rabbinic literature helps Christians unpack the meaning of the word as we now understand it. *Shalom* means wholeness, completeness,[4] healthiness, intactness of the community.[5] This two-syllable word can hold inside it the concept of totality.[6]

Author and activist Lisa Sharon Harper puts it this way:

From Genesis 1 and 2, *shalom* is a vision of a kingdom that provides for all. It is a vision of abundance, of God's presence wiping away fear. It is also a vision of just and healthy interdependent relationships—a vision of respect for the image of God present in all humanity and the call and capacity of all humanity to exercise dominion. What's more, it is a vision of the self-existent, supreme God present and active in the muck with humanity. It is an intimate vision of a genuine love relationship between God and humanity, and that relationship is interconnected with all other relationships in creation.[7]

Shalom is the world as it should be. Shalom is the world in its intended wholeness and perfect totality. Shalom is what humans were created for and what was disrupted by sin. When sin entered the world, it corrupted all creation. Disrupting shalom disrupted the order of all things: our personal presence with God, our relationships with one another, and our connection and care for creation. The rest of the Bible is a journey back to the way we were meant to be as humans on earth with other creatures and all the systems we touch that sustain us. The good news is that the end of the story is just like the beginning.

In the End

If you're like me, then Revelation may as well have been a book of scary stories to read around the campfire. It was a collection of tales of future monsters, beasts, and battles that pointed to the end of our poor planet, and if we were good enough, we might just get to miss that part. Now that I've spent more time in its pages, I have actually come to enjoy talking about the end of the world that Revelation describes, because the end is actually so much better than I imagined. It's not a destruction. It's a radical transformation. I actually squeal with joy to myself and feel hot, joyful tears in my eyes these days when I peek into the end of the Bible, because this is so much better than I had ever hoped. We will finally become all we were meant to be—restored to the original vision of God in the garden.

Let's take a look together.

Then I saw a new heaven and a new earth, for the first heaven and the first earth had passed away, and the sea was no more. And I saw the holy city, the new Jerusalem, coming down out of heaven from God, prepared as a bride adorned for her husband. And I heard a loud voice from the throne saying, "See, the home of God is among mortals. He will dwell with them; they will be his peoples, and God himself will be with them and be their God; he will wipe every tear from their eyes. Death will be no more; mourning and crying and pain will be no more, for the first things have passed away." (Revelation 21:1–4)

I know, I know. Those who see the world being destroyed and remade will use these same verses to prove their point. We read the words "passed away" and make some leaps because of how we tend to use the words in our modern context. However, there are a few reasons why I have come to see it as a restoration and not a destruction: how Paul used this same word, what the Old Testament has to say about new creation, and the resurrected body of Christ.

In 2 Corinthians 5:17, Paul uses a word from the same root for "passed away." From the Greek root *erchomai* (to go), Revelation uses *aperchomai* (to go away, depart) and 2 Corinthians uses *parerchomai* (to pass by or pass away) to talk about how if we are in Christ, we are made new: the old has gone and the new has come. This word doesn't necessarily have the connotations of complete destruction or elimination. It just means something ceases to be as it once was.[8] It has been transformed.

But even beyond this little word, the idea of the new Jerusalem and its restoration can be traced back in Scripture to the Old Testament. If we take a stroll through the last few chapters of Isaiah, we see that the major act of God at the end of days is not one of destruction. Rather, it is one of new creation (Isaiah 65:17–25). The eventual hope of Israel in this time was the restoration of the holy mountain of Zion, which is another way of referring to Jerusalem, where the temple (and God's presence) resided.[9] This is Israel's home—the land which God promised to Abraham and Moses and the land to which God promises to return the people of Israel. In this restored Zion, the Most High is enthroned and dwells among God's people, is creator and defender of the world, and keeps cosmic chaos at bay. The city provides refuge for God's people who there receive God's protection and salvation.

And even in Isaiah, this new Jerusalem was for more than Israelites alone. Isaiah speaks of nations and kings coming to this renewed place to proclaim the praise of God. After peace is established for God's people there, Zion then opens to receive the nations, and thus is populated by the holy people from every place. Those who serve God are welcome there (Isaiah 60).[10] At this point in history, Zion will be free and those within it will practice the perfect justice of God and worship God forever. No longer will it be subject to slavery or will its people face exile to another place (Isaiah 61–62).

This extended passage forms the basis of the various allusions in the New Testament to the new Jerusalem specifically and new creation more generally. In these texts, Jerusalem isn't destroyed. It is restored back to its intended glory, and it is the template that John and Paul use to talk about the future of planet Earth and its people (Romans 8, Galatians 4, Revelation 21).

We see this same arc of restoration in the life, death, and resurrection of Christ. Jesus is fully God and fully man. He is the divine wrapped in human flesh and blood. He has a body and soul. We often look at the work of Christ as rescuing souls, and indeed it was that, but not only that. The work of the cross was to make a way for our souls to remove the marks sin has left. To make it possible to be in communion with God once more, a privilege—no, a purpose—we lost in Eden.

But in that work, souls are not destroyed as they are regenerated. That would be like saying, "Well, this guy here is sick. In order to cure him, we must kill him." Healing doesn't work that way physically, and there doesn't seem to be an indication that it happens that way spiritually, either. It is being "born again," of spirit and of flesh. In Jesus' conversation with Nicodemus in John 3, there are no mentions of dying to make that happen. Just rebirth. In Christ's work, souls are made whole, restored.

We see this in Christ himself, a renewed body in his resurrection. Jesus doesn't come back and leave that bit of his humanity behind. He comes right back into his physical body, scars and all—to live and breathe and walk and also teleport into rooms. Jesus' life on earth after his resurrection is *earthy*. He eats, he teaches, and he even allows himself to be touched by Thomas. He is not a ghost-like presence hovering over the earth now. He is flesh like us. He did not leave his body behind when he ascended into heaven, either. His body is up there along with his soul, in his divine, human glory.

And the promise is for us to be reunited with our bodies after death, as well. That is why so many of those churches in England had cemeteries in their vicinity. When we walk past all the saints who have gone before us there as they wait for resurrection, we are reminded of how you and I await resurrection and renewal of the earth. The work of Jesus was not just to defeat sin for our souls but to kick off new creation that will include our bodies. He is the proof that new creation is coming. The renewal of our spiritual selves is just the first sign. The physical is breaking through, starting with our Savior. Paul talks about this in Romans:

> I consider that the sufferings of this present time are not worth comparing with the glory about to be revealed to us. For the creation waits with eager longing for the revealing of the children of God, for the creation was subjected to futility, not of its own will, but by the will of the one who subjected it, in hope that the creation itself will be set free from its enslavement to decay and will obtain the freedom of the glory of the children of God. We know that the whole creation has been groaning together as it suffers together the pains of labor, and not only the creation, but we ourselves, who have the first fruits of the Spirit, groan inwardly while we wait for adoption, the redemption of our bodies. For in hope we were saved. Now hope that is seen is not hope, for who hopes for what one already sees? But if we hope for what we do not see, we wait for it with patience. (Romans 8:18–25)

God isn't taking a cosmic do-over here. It's more like a makeover. God doesn't redo, God renews. We see it in the pages of Scripture from beginning to end. We're seeing it happen now in and through us. The future is God fully present with God's people, and the completeness and justice of shalom existing in every place. The end is the beginning, minus the conflict.

Earthy, Embodied Hope

I met Nyan at a long lunch table in Southeast Asia. We had been around the local area to get footage of the sights and sounds for the morning. After lunch we were going to be capturing faith and church stories from the people gathered there with us, so we spent our time around the table getting to know everyone and hearing about their lives. At one time, Nyan had been in pain for many years. It seemed his lifelong battle with alcoholism was getting the better of his body and his relationships, both of which were beginning to shut down on him. He couldn't see a way out, and he was even beginning to wonder why he should stick around if he was going to feel like this or worse. His habit of drinking it all away just wasn't cutting it like it used to.

One day a friend came to sit with him, and Nyan shared his struggle and his thoughts. He just needed something to convince him to stay, he said. His friend, one of the only Christians he knew, asked if he could pray for Nyan. Convinced it couldn't hurt, Nyan agreed. They bowed their heads together and prayed that his addiction would be broken and his body would heal from the damage the alcohol had done, and later that evening his friend left and Nyan went to bed.

The next morning he woke up, and for the first time ever, he didn't crave a drink. Day after day passed, and soon he realized that the prayer of his friend had worked. He never wanted a drink again. When I met Nyan, it had been ten years since that day, and not only had he never had another drink, but in that time his body had also healed from the effects of his alcoholism. Not long after that powerful prayer, he started following the God of his friend. Because if his life could be changed like this by one moment, what else might be changed for him and for those around him? How could he share this same healing and restoration to others as his friend had shared with him?

Nyan was now one of a community of Jesus followers who gathered to worship, pray, and act in their community. He wanted to see everyone get the opportunity to heal in whatever way they needed, to live in the fullness of the life available from the God who healed him. For him, the hope wasn't distant. It was real, and it existed in him in a tangible way.

That's the invitation of new creation—to give and to receive healing. It's the opportunity to be made new now and, eventually, for eternity. The resurrection of Jesus is the moment new creation began breaking through, and as we have been made new in Christ, we carry that hope of resurrection and renewal with us to all of creation. This hope isn't mere pie-in-the-sky spirituality. It is down-in-the-dirt physicality too.

Destruction would have us wonder, what is the point? It traps us into thinking we need only "win souls" and that we can do so at whatever cost is necessary. This kind of disembodied hope is what leaves lives and bodies broken in our wake. And it leaves the rest of creation behind too. If what matters is the perfected spiritual state beyond this world, we need not care for the world itself or its people. If it is to be destroyed, we need not care for or repair the soil we walk on or the communities we may harm.

We talked a bit about Nicodemus earlier, and perhaps the most famous Bible verse—John 3:16—is found in that conversation: "For God so loved the world that he gave his only Son, so that everyone who believes in him may not perish but may have eternal life." The word for world here is *kosmos*. It can mean all of humanity, especially as an object of God's love, but it can also mean "the sum total of everything here and now;" in other words, the entire universe.[11] The love of God not only changes us, it changes how we interact with the world. Knowing that God's grand plan isn't to separate me from the world, but rather, to include me in its complete redemption, offers me a much more compelling narrative that aligns with the Jesus I find in the Bible.

I don't have rapture or end of the world anxiety anymore. I don't worry about the monsters and mayhem of Revelation either, because I kept reading the story and I see now that God is making us whole again. To believe in restoration is to heed the call back to shalom. It is to understand the importance to every bit of good we do while we're here—not just the spiritual stuff. It means we are connected to others and to creation itself in a joint destiny of renewal. And as people who have become part of Christ and partaken in the spiritual renewal, we are tasked with bringing heaven to earth and being a part of the physical renewal of everything here—nature, relationships, and systems. None of it will be out of the purview of God and God's people on the journey back to shalom.

In these intervening days between when new creation first broke through and when it will be made complete, we get to participate in its purpose. As those who belong to the God of the Bible, we are the ones who hold the whole story and the way to full healing—physical and spiritual. We give up so much if we let the rest of the world care for the physical while we trample through attempting to care for the spiritual. In reality, we need both, because we are both and we will always be both. Caring for the *kosmos* in its wholeness is a supreme act of faith as a disciple of the One who has gone before us. Nothing we do toward that purpose will be wasted. And maybe it's not about whether things get worse before they get better but that they do get better.

FIVE

Kingdom of Good

"**TO BE FROM** my country is to be Muslim," Kerem said with complete seriousness and deep sadness. And it was true. It was more than the societal norm. In our conversation, he shared how for Muslims in his Middle Eastern country, religion was intertwined with everything—education, daily life, the government. National identity was so closely connected to religion that to step away from Islam and into a different faith meant to choose a life of either secrecy or emotional distance from everything and everyone in your life. A few years earlier he had made that difficult decision, and it cost him dearly.

Kerem's journey toward Jesus began slowly, with an acquaintance inviting him for coffee and conversation. Over time, their friendship grew, and so did Kerem's curiosity about Christ, until one day, he just knew. He knew that even though it would mean losing part of his identity, he was ready to follow Jesus. But to turn away from Islam was to have most of the people he knew turn their backs on him—from his family to his friends.

Removed from his home and from the social circles he once inhabited, making it hard to get a job or even find people he trusted in the community, Kerem still trusted he made the right decision. But his friend who introduced him to Christ helped him find a new community in the church in his city. Together they existed in a parallel society with the one that surrounded them, the one that directed the lives of everyone around them.

Just months, maybe even mere weeks, after I flew home from the Middle East where I met Kerem and others, a bomb went off in their capital city's airport as part of an attempted military coup that ultimately failed. As I watched news about the event, I had knots in my stomach, knowing I had stood in that same airport where people lost their lives. I kept thinking about how precarious a more authoritarian government could be, even one operating in the name of the religion that most everyone in that country professed and supported. This dream of an intertwined national and religious identity didn't bring peace in this case. It brought force, exclusion, and alienation from some within and many outside the country's borders.

In the white American evangelical circles I grew up in, there was an assumption that America was God's chosen nation, and that our role as Christians was to make this nation Christian in leadership and law. The teachers and preachers I learned from in my early Christian education continually communicated their dream of an intertwined national and religious identity. Their version wouldn't have been structured like the one I witnessed in the Middle East, but it did strike me that even if one could more or less make your religion and its related moral code a requirement—both legally and culturally—that it may not have the effect or the security desired. I now recognized how harmful it could be to the religious identity to inseparably bind it to the national identity. It did not secure peace. It disrupted peace. It did not create flourishing. It may have impeded flourishing.

The dream of America as *the* Christian nation drove many of my faith community's public efforts, like boycotting brands that supported LGBTQ rights and electing officials based solely on their anti-abortion stances. We believed that our goal was to shape America into the one nation in all the world that embodied the kingdom of God on earth. In doing so we would bring prosperity to America's people and be light to the world. This kind of thinking blurred the lines between the kingdom of God and the American dream of dominance until the two were indistinguishable.

As it turns out, this dominion-seeking in the name of God is part of the history of American evangelicalism, all the way back to the beginning. Many early Americans, who had come to the country for explicitly religious reasons, saw the win over Britain in the American Revolution as a sign of God's special affection for America and its status as a chosen nation who has favor with God in order to spread both evangelical Christianity and democracy.[1] Since then, segments of American Christianity have been especially focused on not just spreading the gospel but obtaining influence in order to mandate Christianity in public spaces.

The driving force behind some of these tendencies today appears to come out of a movement based on what is called the

"Seven Mountains Mandate." This was a purported prophecy delivered by prominent Christian leaders in 1975 declaring the need for the church to invade the seven key mountains of influence in society: education, religion, family, business, government, entertainment, and media.

This movement found a home mostly within more charismatic expressions of American Christianity, but it has also found its way into many mainstream evangelical expressions of Christianity, including the one in which I grew up. It helped lay a battle plan for the culture wars we fought in hope of winning dominance in all these spheres and thus claiming them for God.[2] The idea was that if we could obtain power and use it to change the rules to reflect Christian ethics, we would be helping to establish the kingdom and God would increase the blessings on America.

This framework assumes a world where the only change that happens comes from the top down and where the main goal is nominal belief, personal prosperity, and control of others based on Christian religious values. An extreme example of this thinking today is Christian nationalism, which is a belief that America was founded as a Christian nation and that church and state should not be separate, but that civic life and religious life—specifically Christianity—should be fused together.[3]

This movement tends to turn God's kingdom into a worldly empire (and a particularly American one). And when it does that, it tends to focus on seeking our own greatness—in power and prosperity—instead of our goodness as a people. But that's not really how God's kingdom works. In fact, given our cultural baggage, kingdom may not even be the right word to describe what God intends.

A King, Not a Kingdom

I don't know about you, but when I hear the word *kingdom*, my mind instantly flits to medieval England, to images of a mythical King Arthur on a throne in Camelot ruling courageously and graciously. The word also makes me think of borders and boundaries. In the United States, for example, we know where state lines are and where our nation ends and Mexico or Canada begins. The United States may not be a monarchy, but like a kingdom, the area ruled is clearly defined (though looking through history, those lines have often been less stable).

However, the term *kingdom* here comes from the word *basilea* in Greek, which denotes a reign more than an area to be reigned. Think *kingship* more than *kingdom*. The kingdom of God, then, is more related to the kingship of God than it is to any clearly defined territory. The reign of God has been initiated with Christ's life, death, and resurrection.[4] In this kingdom of God, we are not in charge. God is. There are no borders to defend or people to control. There's a king to serve.

This is part of what makes the kingdom of God so difficult to wrap our minds around. It's less obvious, less organized, and less attractive by the world's standards. Even the disciples struggled with this bit. They expected the Messiah to come as a conquering hero king, the kind who would kick out whichever empire was oppressing them at the time and restore Israel as the powerful nation it was meant to be. And to be fair, for Israel, the physical and spiritual rule of God *were* all mixed up together. Their political lines for their promised land and their religion were tied together. And for them, this made sense because of their covenant with the Lord.

So Jesus really threw everyone for a loop. When God Incarnate instead arrived in the form of a poor carpenter from Bethlehem, the story didn't quite play out the way anyone expected. It took some time to realize that the kingdom, too, would not be like anyone expected. The national borders no longer applied in the same way because Jesus opened the doors to invite everyone in. So how does one talk about a kingdom without talking about who, where, or what is in its area of rule?

It's no wonder, then, that we struggle to interpret or define what the kingdom is or what it means. It doesn't help that Jesus often refused to give straight answers to questions asked of him. The gospels all include accounts of Jesus declaring the good news that the kingdom of God was near, but in true Jesus form, he preferred to talk about it in parables. This frustrated and perplexed a lot of people, including his disciples. Even in Matthew 13, when they directly ask him why he uses parables, he responds that many people are not ready for the answers. So he communicates through parables so that only those who are ready and willing to unpack the "secrets of the kingdom" can understand what he's saying (Matthew 13:13). It was also to fulfill prophecy because many would see and hear and yet not understand (Isaiah 6:9–10). Jesus was following the plan laid out from the beginning.

Jesus also understood and harnessed the power of storytelling—sometimes we cannot describe a thing outright, or at least not well. There are ideas and concepts that we can only describe with metaphor or simile. A storyteller can attach an unfamiliar concept to something we do know and understand so the listeners can glimpse it in part. This is especially true when it comes to the things of God, who is far beyond our human understanding. There is mystery inherent in such concepts. But using what has been revealed to us about the world and God is one helpful way we find a vocabulary to describe the divine and mysterious.

Parables use the familiar to describe the unfamiliar, but often Jesus puts an unusual twist on the idea in order to engage the hearer, prompt a response, and leave space for doubts and questions to be pondered in the story's wake.[5] Through these stories, Jesus helped draw attention to the nuances of the kingdom in ways that prompted processing of what this new way of living would mean for everyone there.

Outside the Lines

In Matthew 13, we see a whole string of parables about the kingdom of God, and in them we learn some key lessons about how the kingdom grows, how we ought to respond to encountering it, and how we may not easily draw lines around who and where are a part of it. Let's take a look together.

Parable of the Sower: Matthew 13:1-9, 18-23

This parable describes the many kinds of ground that seed can fall on when being planted—rocky ground, thorns, and good soil—and how each kind of environment affects its growth. Jesus explains that each kind of soil represents a heart ready to receive the seed of the message of God's rule, but though that seed may be ready to do its job in the moment, many enemies seek to keep the seed from taking root and producing fruit. Society, pressure, wealth, or other distractions may come in and hinder the seed from producing the fruit of a life under God's rule. Most of those who receive the message don't return with good fruit. So many will hear of the kingdom but not all will receive the message and live under the rule of God. This is not a kingdom that comes through force. It springs up only in the ground that is ready to receive it.

Parable of Weeds among the Wheat: Matthew 13:24-30, 36-43

In this parable a man sows wheat seeds in his field, but the enemy sneaks in to plant something else in the same soil: weeds. So when the seeds begin to grow, and the sower can finally see what fruit will come of the seeds he's sown, he finds weeds alongside wheat in the soil he cultivated. He then decides to wait it out and have the reapers separate the plants after all are harvested.

Here Jesus was describing how both weeds and wheat grow together—the desired plants of God's kingdom like justice, holiness, and goodness, and the undesired plants of the enemy like injustice, sin, and evil. The success of each is not based on how well it grows, nor does it help the crop of good to seek the destruction of evil while the good is growing into maturity. Both will exist until the day of harvest. It's not a game of numbers but of quality, and when the day comes, the quality of the plant will determine its fate. Justice, holiness, and goodness will remain, but injustice, sin, and evil—the seeds of the enemy—will be destroyed. What will be left in God's kingdom is only the just, holy, and good.

Parable of the Mustard Seed: Matthew 13:31-32

This parable is short and sweet. The kingdom is like a mustard seed, which starts very small, but will grow into a big shrub or tree. What begins as a tiny seed can become a place of refuge for the birds. The kingdom has unexpected roots. It may even look insignificant in the beginning, but it becomes a sanctuary to those who need it. We cannot always tell in the beginning what something will become. Whether it is the small nation of ancient Israel or the ragtag team of disciples that followed Jesus, the roots of the kingdom were not impressive to many on the outside. But as we move through history, we'll see that the kingdom grows wide and provides refuge and sustenance for those who need it.

Parable of the Yeast: Matthew 13:33

In this parable, we see another small something—yeast—make a difference in a big way. Here the woman in focus mixes a little yeast with a lot of flour. It may not seem like enough proportionally, but it turns out that all of the bread was leavened because of the effect of the yeast. God's kingdom will influence every part of the normal world, and it will often do so in unexpected and undetected ways. We won't see it happen. It will be under the surface and mixed in with all the other ingredients, but once it's ready, we cannot escape its effects.

Parable of the Treasure: Matthew 13:44

Here a man finds a treasure in a field. He then hides it, and he sells everything he owns and buys the field to possess this treasure. Here we have shifted from the invisible nature of the kingdom of God to its value and effect on our lives. This man gives up everything he has for a hidden treasure of great value. Finding this treasure disrupted his entire life, and like him, when we wholeheartedly commit to the kingdom, our lives are disrupted and the only wise response is to sacrifice our normal life, patterns, and possessions to be a part of it. It doesn't seem wise to those who don't know its value, but for those of us who do, it's the only thing that makes sense.

Parable of the Pearl: Matthew 13:45–46

In this parable, Jesus describes a merchant specifically looking for a valuable pearl. Upon finding a pearl that has great value, the merchant sells everything. Much like the parable of the treasure, the person who discovers something of value sacrifices much in order to obtain it. However, the merchant in this story didn't stumble upon the pearl. They were deliberately searching for it, and they didn't find many pearls. They found one pearl. This connects to the example of the good soil from the earlier parable—the one who is ready and searching for the right thing finds it, and when it is found, that person acts accordingly.

This parable is about what our response to encountering the kingdom of God should look like. We can spend our lives looking for what matters, and this parable shows us what to do when we find it in the kingdom of God. We run; we don't walk. We give everything to it because it is worth that much. The kingdom of God doesn't necessarily demand that of us, but we would be wise to give it.

Parable of the Net: Matthew 13:47–50

Here the kingdom of God is like a net that is thrown out of a boat and captures every kind of fish. At some point the good and the bad fish must be separated from each other, as with the wheat and the weeds. Shifting to the kingdom parallel, Jesus says that in the end, the angels will separate the good from the bad and send them to their destinies—but until then we are here together.

The kingdom of God is like the net—not the fish, not the fisherman, but the net. The net of the kingdom is cast wide. It captures every kind of fish. There is no separating ourselves as the people of God completely or even telling for sure who among us will be considered among the "good" fish when the time comes. Those within the kingdom are not defined by a particular "kind." Every kind of fish is sought and welcomed, and it is again the quality of the fish—decided by the standards of God implemented through the angels—that determines their destiny. There will be a sorting, but we don't get to be the deciders. We don't get to put our own guidelines and restrictions on who gets in or out, or what kind of action is deemed good or bad (although we may have some guesses based on Scripture). In the end, I have a feeling the scope of the kingdom will probably surprise us all.

Jesus then summarizes the purpose of sharing all these parables in verse 52: "Therefore every scribe who has become a disciple in the kingdom of heaven is like the master of a household who brings out of his treasure what is new and what is old." Here he's saying that with these parables the hearers have the new ideas alongside the old. In Matthew 5:17, Jesus says that he didn't come to abolish the Law but to fulfill it. He is not saying that what has come before is obsolete. Rather it is in continuity with what God began in Israel and expanded in Christ. The kingship of God began in Israel, and it is not gone there. The covenant God made with the Jewish people remains, but there is also a new covenant in Christ. It is when we put the two together that we see the full scope of God's work in history then, now, and forever.

When Jesus describes the kingdom, the focus is less on where it is and what it looks like than on our response to the good news that God reigns. There are no particular borders or rules placed on it. You may not even detect the kingdom growing, but you will know where it touches: wherever you see God's people responding to God's rule. Instead we see that the kingdom is valuable, is a refuge, includes every kind of person, and only the good, just, and holy will dwell in it eternally.

The kingdom is not about turning the world into our empire in God's name. It is not about climbing our way to greatness. It is about cultivating a life and community of goodness. That is what stands in the end. The kingship of God is displayed now in how we choose to live under God's rule and in the future when the kingdom has come in its fullness—the kingdom of good. But those who seek to live in the kingdom of good will find it often has ramifications, and if we are to take Jesus seriously, those ramifications are unlikely to look like our dominion or prosperity.

#Blessed

"Hey girl!" If you're a millennial woman, that greeting may have induced an involuntary response in you, and if you're not, let me explain. I don't know what happened, but sometime in the 2010s, multi-level marketing companies made a comeback in a big way. As a millennial woman myself, I couldn't scroll through my social media feeds without seeing another friend hawking body wraps, leggings, beauty products, or nutritional supplements. Then a message would pop up from a friend I hadn't talked to in literally years and, for some reason, it almost always began with "Hey girl!" The public posts and private messages were often filled with all the successes—big and small—this new company, product, or lifestyle had brought them. Inevitably, they would end the post with a list of hashtags, always including #blessed. Describing yourself as "#blessed" has become something of a joke now, but it started in this very real place.

The idea of blessing is not foreign to the Christian life. The Bible often shares what brings blessing and what doesn't. Psalm 1, for example, lists several characteristics and actions that are considered blessed. So I'm not ready to throw #blessed under the bus, but we also need to be clear that what we identify as "blessed" is less "boss babe" and more biblical. The biblical idea of blessing is very different from the prosperity promises we encounter, and we see this at work perhaps most clearly in the Beatitudes in the Sermon on the Mount.

Overwhelmingly, the Sermon on the Mount focuses on the kingdom of heaven. (Or the kingdom of God—but with this language the book's author, Matthew, is likely being sensitive to his primarily Jewish readers, who wouldn't say the name of God.)[6] Jesus is teaching his people how to live as part of his kingdom of heaven as they walk on earth together.

In a striking parallelism to the ten commandments in Exodus, where God began marking out the rules for flourishing, Jesus walks to the top of a mountain, full of divine authority, and lays out nine beatitudes that display the priorities and promises of the people who would be called God's own. If in the parables of Matthew 13, which we discussed earlier in this chapter, we see that the kingdom is worth giving up everything for, here in the Beatitudes we see what we get when we go all in (Matthew 5).

Each line in the Beatitudes begins with the Greek word *makarios*. This word usually gets translated as happy, blessed, or favored. Typically, that word is a mental marker for the audience for a sign of flourishing. Whatever is listed after "blessed" is often the cause of the blessing.[7] For the Greeks, they would expect outward markers like wealth, many children, or successful ventures to be listed as signs they were flourishing.[8] In Jewish culture, a sign of flourishing would more likely be tied to inner markers like their relationship to God or holiness.[9] Knowing the expectations, then, it's clear to see that in the Beatitudes themselves, the audience does not quite get what they expect, and it's probably not what we would expect either.

What we see in the list Jesus gives is the values of the kingdom of heaven. In each line, there is something a person who is part of the kingdom should embody or expect, followed by a future hope which is the basis for their blessing. In this passage, Jesus lists a series of circumstances that we would never identify as happy or blessed by earthly terms, yet he describes the person as flourishing even and especially then because of the future hope of the kingdom. In the chart on the next page, I've broken out the signs of flourishing (the blessed characteristic) and the future hope on which the flourishing stands.

As you take a look at the chart, notice what's missing from these signs of flourishing: money, family, status, and power—the markers that Greek culture (like ours) would have associated with favor. Instead, Jesus suggests that in his kingdom, favor lies with those who are poor in spirit (despairing or depending on others),[10] mourning, or meek (those who do not seek to lord over others).[11] As Jesus moves through the list, he also emphasizes the inner postures traditionally valued in his Jewish tradition: a hunger and thirst for righteousness (or justice), mercy, and purity of heart (those who seek

Current Signs of Flourishing in the Kingdom	Future Hope of the Kingdom for Flourishing
Poor in spirit	Theirs is the kingdom of heaven
Those who mourn	They will be comforted
The meek	They will inherit the earth
Those who hunger and thirst for righteousness	They will be filled
Merciful	They will receive mercy
Pure in heart	They will see God
Peacemakers	They will be called children of God
Persecuted for the sake of righteousness	Theirs is the kingdom of heaven
When people revile, persecute, and utter evil against you	Your reward will be great in heaven

God above the world's temptations and comforts). This is how we ought to order our relationships to one another. We seek the world to be set right. We practice mercy as God practiced mercy on us, and we seek to live the values of heaven rather than valuing the status seeking on earth.

In the end, this is all wrapped up in one word: peacemaking. That is the integrated action that brings all of the Beatitudes together. This is where our inner postures meet our outer actions. Blessed are those who actively work to reconcile people and the wrong done between them, because they will be counted as the family of God when the kingdom comes in full.

This is not the kind of relentless happiness that defines toxic positivity or the kind of superficial blessing that describes a windfall of material possessions or favorable circumstances.

We may not appear to be #blessed. Abundance and peace for all in the future kingdom of God is our promise, but while we wait for that day and live by those values in this moment, we can expect a life that might not look to the world like flourishing. We will be falsely accused and maybe even physically hurt because of our commitment to Christ and to living out those values. Real persecution comes because of our commitment to righteousness, to justice, to living the life of the coming kingdom today—not because of our success, money, power, or influence. Quite the opposite: we may find ourselves persecuted because we lack those things, because we live in defiance to the very idea that they are the values that give our lives meaning and importance. And in all that difficulty, we are marked by our hope.

I stood on the chilly gray stone floors of the Notre-Dame de Paris Cathedral one summer day about eight years ago. I moved slowly through each area of the church—drinking in the rose windows, high arches, and other features that made my jaw actually hang open the entire time. As I moved to the center of the cathedral, I saw rows and rows of chairs set out. Hundreds of people were probably crammed into the church to take in the artistry, but only a handful sat in the chairs to pray. It struck me how the original builders of such a grand place would feel to see it now. It was full, but not of pilgrims and pray-ers. We were tourists visiting another historical place—the house of God. Though full of the creativity handed down to us by our Creator God, it was left hollow of spiritual presence and purpose . . . at least for the afternoon.

France and other nations in Europe are often called post-Christian, because though they were historically shaped by Christian institutions, leaders, and traditional values, the way their citizens live and engage in life is no longer guided by practicing Christianity.[12] Centuries of these nation-state-aligned churches seeking greatness did not lead where they wanted it to, and it may have even led to a whole lot less goodness because sometimes the "greater good" for us blinds us to the "common good" for all.

At one time, I believed that my role as a follower of Christ was to fight for every inch of influence I could get in order to make the kingdom of God real on earth. Doing this required enforcing the moral code that was handed down to me on those around me, and if I could do that, then I was not only doing "kingdom work" but I would thrive because of it. I look back now, and I see how this thinking put me and those like me at the top of the pyramid, but that's not how the Bible shows us that it works.

The kingship of God puts God at the center. Our role is to respond. It's not about what we get or how others respond. It's about how we go about living the values of the kingdom every day. I don't need my nation to fall in line with Christian values to make an impact, and I don't need to push my way to the top to be #blessed. Domination is not the central work of the church for God. Goodness is. Peacemaking is. Reconciliation is. Wholeness is. When the church seeks the goodness and flourishing of the world—in the small, quiet ways as much as the big, systemic ones—we find our own flourishing along the way. That's the kind of kingdom I want to live in.

SIX

Understanding Our Family Legacy

I WAS WALKING through the ruins of a Hindu temple in Southeast Asia, and it felt like I had just finished a big puzzle—but some of the pieces were still left over. The country is now a majority Muslim country, but it wasn't always that way. Hinduism had the upper hand for most of its existence. This temple was one of the last major remnants of that past. Stones were stacked upon other stones for as high as ten or fifteen stories. The once white stone now had turned to gray, and was overgrown by moss that provided contrast to the vibrant blue sky behind it.

We would be spending the afternoon in a home recording stories of people in the local home churches, but on these trips, we didn't just sit in rooms and listen to stories. The rest of the time, we were getting footage of major sites or parts of daily life for those who live there. This morning we were being the typical tourists and exploring the ruins. Among its visitors that day were little kids on field trips and older women in their richly colored hijabs.

The reassembled building was only one part of the site. Right next to it was what looked like a sculpture garden, with bits of stone rebuilt into small structures or strewn about in a semi-orderly fashion. These were the parts of the temple that didn't get put back into the structure that people were now climbing up and exploring. As it turns out, this temple has actually been rebuilt a time or two. Each time, an earthquake had shaken the structure to its core and taken it down. Each time, some of the fallen pieces broke, so they had to rebuild the temple in a way that made sense of the pieces they had now. Now it served as a popular tourist attraction that helped tell the story of the past. It was carved in stone, built to last forever, and yet had proved delicate enough to pass away.

As we drove away from the ruins that day, I couldn't help but place the present Christian movements we were seeing take place in this part of the world alongside the temple of religion past. This culture was so inhospitable to Christians that the church there actually hid in plain sight. The group of believers we met with most often had cobbled together a new kind of family—each having been alienated in some way from their own. One was disowned by his parents, another became an outcast as his school, and several of the girls still lived at home and wore their hijabs while sneaking out to worship Jesus without their parents' knowledge. This group of people met most often in a classroom at a nearby school because one of them was a teacher there, but it wasn't the only place they came together. Coffee shops, front stoops, soccer pitches, and public parks all became spaces for community and connection for this church when needed. Unlike the temples and mosques spread across this island country, this church couldn't be knocked down or destroyed, and because it was everywhere and nowhere, it also couldn't be contained. There's something beautiful about an idea of community that extends beyond time and space.

Later that same year, the church I was a member of announced a capital campaign. This phrase, borrowed from the corporate world, usually refers to raising money for a new building—asking members to commit more money, on top of general giving, to a specific goal. Ours was for renovations to better use our space, but it still felt a little weird to me. Perhaps I wouldn't have thought anything of it before. It's hard to say. Since I became an adult and a donor to my church community, I had never been part of a capital campaign before. That trip to Southeast Asia wasn't the first time I saw the unconventional gathering places of churches, but suddenly, the contrast between the realities of the global church and the realities of many American churches was hitting very close to home. I didn't know how to respond to the big ask for a commitment to a building.

I didn't see the church building as the most central space for the Christian life anymore. Before some of these experiences overseas, in my mind, the church was a location, a gathering place. But now I don't think of church as a place—it is people and practices bound by the blood of Christ. And it wasn't just about the people or the place but also the work of the church. Is the best use of our resources to bring people to this building? Is that where ministry mainly happens for most of us? Does this funding focus mean that we concentrate on drawing people in more than sending people out?

Has something like that ever prompted you to rethink what you thought church is or ought to be? What we do and why we're there? I wasn't sure how I felt or what I wanted to do about it. It meant my husband and I had to process more than what we could afford to give. We needed to think more deeply about what church isn't, what it is, what it can be, and what that meant for our role in community. And that's what we're going to explore more together in this chapter.

Beyond Sunday Morning

As a Christian in Christian spaces online and offline, I find myself in conversations with friends about what's happening in our lives, and church comes up regularly. Whether we worship in the same local church or different ones, I find that our language about church reflects some of the limited ways we think about it. I hear (and have probably said) things like . . .

- "We have church at that time so we won't be able to make it."

- "I guess we'll have to miss church this week because we've got this other thing."

- "We have church first, but after that my day is wide open."

Comments like these reveal a belief that church is a weekly event and not something we embody—that it's a to-do list item instead of a to-be list item. This kind of thinking compartmentalizes our faith from everything else. But this mentality isn't just wrong, it's actually hindering us from embodying the purpose of church and benefiting from it too. The Bible talks very little about what happens in a weekly worship service, specifically. Most of what we call "church" is actually tradition—beautiful and powerful, yes, but still tradition, and often tradition that we don't even agree on from one denomination to another.

When the Bible talks about church, it doesn't read like a "how to have a worship service" blog post. Instead, Paul and others enlisted the help of metaphors to provide instruction about how to be and do church. By doing so, they painted a picture of church that extends beyond weekly gatherings into a worship that touches every part of our lives.

Worship isn't just singing, preaching, or praying (alone or in private). It's meant to extend into our whole lives, and that whole life is about sacrifice.[1] By limiting church to this one place and the worship and study we do there, we miss the opportunity to see it as part of our calling. This mentality keeps us from being seen, supported, and spiritually formed . . . and doing the same for others.

When we grasp the meaning behind the metaphors, we see that we are a deeply interconnected people capable of bringing our worship into unexpected spaces and circumstances. Let's explore the metaphors the New Testament writers used to capture the meaning of church and how they can expand our vision of what this calling looks like in our lives.

Temple

For through him both of us have access in one Spirit to the Father. So then, you are no longer strangers and aliens, but you are fellow citizens with the saints and also members of the household of God, built upon the foundation of the apostles and prophets, with Christ Jesus himself as the cornerstone; in him the whole structure is joined together and grows into a holy temple in the Lord, in whom you also are built together spiritually into a dwelling place for God. (Ephesians 2:18–22)

Come to him, a living stone, though rejected by mortals yet chosen and precious in God's sight, and like living stones let yourselves be built into a spiritual house, to be a holy priesthood, to offer spiritual sacrifices acceptable to God through Jesus Christ. For it stands in scripture: "See, I am laying in Zion a stone, a cornerstone chosen and precious, and whoever believes in him will not be put to shame." (1 Peter 2:4–6)

In the Hebrew Bible (what many Christians call the Old Testament), the temple was the place where God dwelled, and only a priest could come near to God in the holy of holies. But because of the Holy Spirit, the temple now resides in God's people. We are the place where God dwells. Each person is a living stone that, together with others, creates a sacred space. We have a foundation that is built on the proclamations of the apostles and aligned with the Son. We are the building placed brick by brick by God. We are designed to be together, and we're continually being built up by one another.

By drawing on the imagery of the temple, the authors show us that when we come together, we bring God with us. We don't need that to be once a week or even in a specific place. That's part of what we all bring to the church—the presence of Godself—and we exist to bring that presence to each other and the world.

Body

> For just as the body is one and has many members, and all
> the members of the body, though many, are one body, so
> it is with Christ. For in the one Spirit we were all baptized
> into one body—Jews or Greeks, slaves or free—and we
> were all made to drink of one Spirit. Indeed, the body does
> not consist of one member but of many. (1 Corinthians
> 12:12–14)

The human body is complex. Each of our bodies has parts
on the outside and systems on the inside, all carefully placed
and fine-tuned to operate as a whole. After the passage quoted
above, Paul goes on to say that a body can't work as just one
ear or as one eye . . . nor can we say that a hand doesn't belong.
In other words, our gifts, our backgrounds, and our resources
are perfectly calibrated to help the body operate optimally.

Each part of the body is vital. When one part shuts down
or breaks, the rest suffer. Part of being the church means
using your gifts, your experiences, and your resources for
the building up of the body and for others. Church is not a
moment but a mission, and it's one we are meant to work
together to fulfill all the time—not just on Sundays.

Priesthood

In the Hebrew Bible, priests were the designated class of people who could perform the ritualistic duties that cleansed the
Israelites and made it possible for them to have communion
with God through sacrifices. They were also the only ones
who could go into sections of the temple, and only the high
priest could go into the holy of holies. Before he did so, he
had to perform a sacrifice for his own purification just to be

with God.[2] But through the work of Christ and the anointing of the Holy Spirit, no such barriers to God need exist. In the same way, there are no longer limits on who can do the work of the Lord among his people.

> But you are a chosen people, a royal priesthood, a holy nation, God's own people, in order that you may proclaim the excellence of him who called you out of darkness into his marvelous light. (1 Peter 2:9)

> They sing a new song: "You are worthy to take the scroll and to break its seals, for you were slaughtered and by your blood you ransomed for God saints from every tribe and language and people and nation; you have made them a kingdom and priests serving our God, and they will reign on earth." (Revelation 5:9–10)

In these passages we see that priesthood is not just for Israel, and it's not just for a class of leaders of certain bloodlines or education. It's for each of us. We are all priests now.

> The doctrine of the priesthood of all believers states that all believers in Christ share in his priestly status; therefore, there is no special class of people who mediate the knowledge, presence, and forgiveness of Christ to the rest of believers, and all believers have the right and authority to read, interpret, and apply the teachings of Scripture.
> —J. V. Fesko[3]

We see this truth play out on the pages of the New Testament and in our lives every day. People who once persecuted the church like Paul or denied association with Jesus and tried to solve problems with a sword like Peter or had successful businesses like Lydia or small businesses like Aquila and Priscilla—these are the men and women God used to spread the gospel, perform miracles, and encourage and correct other believers. All did so because of the Holy Spirit working through them. That same Holy Spirit lives in us and gives us all we need for what is asked of us as believers.

But with that gift also comes the responsibility of mediating God's purpose and presence in the lives of others. Spiritual formation is the responsibility of the community. God forms us into disciples through each other. This is a duty that can't be performed once a week on a mass level. It must be a lived-out calling through the community. Together we become better disciples, but it takes all of us.

From Consumption to Kinship

Once upon a time, I owned my own business. I was a professional marketer for personal brands, helping them achieve all the buzzword goals: grow your audience, increase your engagement, increase revenue and retention, and turn customers into advocates. I should have noticed it earlier, but in doing this work it dawned on me that a lot of churches operated with these same goals: grow attendance, convert attendees to members, increase tithes and monthly giving, and turn members into advocates for your church. Now, don't get me wrong. These can be *fine* goals, and they even measure some of the areas that churches need to pay attention to, like member engagement, sustainability, and mission. But it got really weird listening to churches articulate their big visions and realizing that they felt all too similar to the visions of the CEOs with whom I worked closely. Church had started to orient itself a bit like a business. I quickly realized it wasn't just churches, either—it was also the myriad industries that arose around evangelicalism, like music, publishing, and events. Author Skye Jethani calls this the evangelical industrial complex (EIC).[4]

Though many churches may begin down this path with good intentions—perhaps driven by a hope that by adopting these best practices they can better do the work God has called them to do—these different industries and their strategies didn't just change how church was done from the leadership perspective. This mindset also changes the dynamic of those who attend churches or participate in the EIC. Now instead of disciples—those who learn and live in the way of Jesus—we have a whole lot of consumers looking for a place to fulfill their desires instead of a place that turns them into people who fulfill the needs of the world around them.

When we adopt a consumer model for our churches, we tend to define our vision and goals only by what brings people in or makes them feel good (because that is what brings them back). How does this show up in churches and create dynamics that keep people from being fully formed disciples of Christ? One dynamic the church may adopt is that of a club, a primarily social space. It feels more like a fraternity or sorority. Some values and rituals bind us, and we have some shared philanthropic pursuits. But in this model, people didn't really join for all of that. They joined because it seemed fun and like cool people were there who they'd want to know and network with. They felt at home, which is a good thing. The other members became their friends, which is also

All good things

a good thing, but really the club dynamic is the point and not just a part of the whole.

The consumer-driven approach also can also result in churches that operate like a classroom. I know I tend to gravitate towards churches like this. There is so much to learn—again, a good thing—and this kind of church really focuses on handing down the knowledge they feel is important. In this church, attendees leave with a lot of new information but with very few concrete ways or opportunities to turn that into personal and community transformation.

Churches can also choose to focus more on experience or emotion—a conference-style approach. These churches want people to have what feels like an encounter with God, and build an experience meant to facilitate that. Sometimes attendees do indeed experience an authentic connection, but sometimes it's the key change in the music, the fog machines, and the self-help-adjacent sermons—again, all intentionally nurtured to evoke a specific reaction—that have produced that feeling. People in this church feel really good walking out of that church, but the experience stays there in the building, in the room, and not in them as they go out into the world.

Finally, we have what is the most dangerous dynamic: cult. These churches are built around charismatic leaders. People go there because they are looking for proximity to someone important or someone doing important things. Often the pastors are full of hot takes and hard truths that happen to align with what the people in the pews already believe. The connections between the people are often cultivated through a focus on "us versus them." These churches help fuel personal empires, and all who step in the way of that goal find themselves pushed down or pushed out.

Sometimes a church will check boxes in more than one category, and to be fair, these dynamics don't only exist in evangelical churches. But while churches may have some good intentions in adopting models that lead to most of these toxic church dynamics, none of them encompass all of what Scripture and history show us that the church really is.

The earliest church members as described in Acts understood the assignment. Shaped by the idea of church drawn out in the metaphors we discussed above, once they were incorporated by baptism they let church permeate their entire lives:

> They devoted themselves to the apostles' teaching and fellowship, to the breaking of bread and the prayers. Awe came upon everyone because many wonders and signs were being done through the apostles. All who believed were together and had all things in common; they would sell their possessions and goods and distribute the proceeds to all, as any had need. Day by day, as they spent much time together in the temple, they broke bread at home and ate their food with glad and generous hearts, praising God and having the goodwill of all the people. And day by day the Lord added to their number those who were being saved. (Acts 2:42–47)

This passage identifies four main activities that defined the early church:

- *Worship* – "breaking of bread and prayers" indicates some of the spiritual rituals they participated in together, like communion. This act of remembrance and worship was important to their daily practice.

- *Proclamation* – "devoted to the apostles' teaching" shows that they took what the apostles told them about Jesus and the new kingdom seriously, and that they not only heard it but understood and acted on it, as the rest of Acts shows us.

- *Service* – "sold their possessions and goods and distributed the proceeds to all as any had need" shows that they sought to aid one another as much as possible, and we see this go beyond their own circles and into the marginalized parts of the society around them in the rest of Acts too.

- *Fellowship* – "spent much time together, ate food with glad and generous hearts" as well as the distribution of possessions shows that they were a part of each other's daily lives. Church was no checklist event or passing activity. It was a community that took a share in the lives of those within it.

Wherever the church is participating in these functions, it is participating in the legacy of the earliest church that carries us forward to today. It is . . .

- The church meeting quietly in someone's home, made of a few families learning what it means to follow Christ together

- The communion of saints in a glorious cathedral singing psalms, joining together in liturgical prayers, and being sent into their communities to care for others

- A Sunday school class where people who love Christ are challenged to be accountable and to do the work of justice in the world

- The small group that meets during the month to learn, laugh, and love together

- The prayer group that meets every week in secret because they live in an inhospitable nation, but the members conspire to care for their neighbors anyway

- The online community of Christians who encourage one another, show each other what it means to love Jesus more, and help to meet tangible needs in each other's lives

Christianity is bigger and wider than our past experiences. It cannot be confined to one place, tradition, or people. It is available and active wherever followers of Jesus gather to worship, fellowship, care, and proclaim the good news. The form is fluid, but the function remains. And wherever we function as the church, we find ourselves in a new kind of family bonded by the blood of Christ.

Growing up as I did in twentieth century America, I was taught to desire the American dream of a suburban house with a picket fence, husband, and 2.5 children. However, that concept of the family hasn't existed for most of the world's history. First there were bands and clans and tribes that were defined by their family, ethnic, or regional connection. These shared connections created a network, a web of people, your extended family of sorts. But it often actually went deeper than that, to a concept called kinship. As cultural commentator David Brooks describes in an article for the *Atlantic* titled "The Nuclear Family Was a Mistake":

For vast stretches of human history people lived in extended families consisting of not just people they were related to but people they chose to cooperate with. . . . Extended families in traditional societies may or may not have been genetically close, but they were probably emotionally closer than most of us can imagine. In a beautiful essay on kinship, Marshall Sahlins, an anthropologist at the University of Chicago, says that kin in many such societies share a "mutuality of being." The late religion scholar J. Prytz-Johansen wrote that kinship is experienced as an "inner solidarity" of souls. . . . Kinsmen belong to one another, Sahlin writes, because they see themselves as "members of one another."[5]

We may bond by blood or location, but we may also bond by surviving a near-death experience, migrating to a new location together, or sharing a prized resource. Imagine then, what it was like for early Christians to be forging ahead together in a new belief system and lifestyle that looked wildly different than the society around them. It was a struggle, and one that might cost Christians their lives at that. Jesus even warned of the division that comes with the truth he proclaimed, the truth we live by. When our loyalties change, our families may as well. It's no surprise then that in the wake of leaving behind the values or beliefs they grew up with, the early Christians found themselves in need of a new family. But as a new group of "kin" forged in the blood of Jesus, the support system they needed could be created.

When I was a kid, my mom, sisters, and I lived with my grandpa for several years. As my mom was a single mother then, we found ourselves in need of support—financially, and in daily tasks, like childcare and house work, because my mom commuted an hour away for work every day. My grandpa let us live in his home, picking us up from school every day and often cooking for us. The church is meant to be that kind of family for each other because we are part of a kin-dom as much as a kingdom.

When we expand our vision of church as more than a building or an event, we realize how responsible we are to and for one another. As the body of Christ, we bear one another's burdens joyfully, and in the process, we thrive together—showing the world what Christ looks like through our self-giving love.

When my definition of church expanded, I began to see all the places that the church has existed beyond my own specific experiences. Our Christian family legacy extends through time and space, across the ages, and around the world. It gave me freedom to change from one tradition to another, knowing that I didn't leave the larger family; I just found a different household within it. We are not defined by our past, and Christianity is not defined by one expression. Rather, we are defined by how we choose to live as kin to one another and in the purposes of God to serve the world. And I can live into that call whether I am at home with my husband, in my local church building, doing work in the community, or sitting in a café on the other side of the world.

SEVEN

The Pain in the Promise

SATYA AND SHYLA are two of the bravest people I've ever met. By most standards, they would be considered rebellious teenage girls. In a culture that values family, obedience, and tradition, they disobeyed their parents and intentionally broke from the path and values that were carved out for them by their community. In their region of South Asia, Hinduism is the only acceptable religion, but one day someone introduced them to Jesus. In a work of the Holy Spirit, they trusted their friend and decided Jesus was worth following. They didn't know it would cost them dearly.

When they told their parents about this exciting development in their lives, they expected to be met with joy, maybe even for their parents to express the same desire to follow Jesus. It did not go that way. It didn't go well at all, in fact. Their parents decided to keep them in their room when they were not in school or with people they knew, away from friends or outside influences. Sometimes they were abused physically and emotionally when they tried to go to the local church.

For Satya and Shyla, the notion of persecution was not far off or theoretical, and still they decided that following Jesus was worth the price of their "rebellion." Eventually, they were kicked out of their home for sneaking out to church and trainings held by local believers, and they were entirely cut off from their family and the financial resources that would sustain them. They were the poor, mourning, and humble, but their church community took them in and cared for them. Jesus continued to be their hope, and they continued to share their hope with others. By the time I met them, they had actually played a part in planting over fifteen house churches. For them, the cost was worth it.

"I don't know what it means to have to give up everything to follow Jesus," I remember saying, probably too honestly, to some friends after sharing stories like these from my encounters with global Christians. It felt a little taboo to say out loud, but I knew they didn't know, either. Growing up in the Bible Belt of the United States, deep in Christian circles, we had no idea what it looked like to stare down everything we had or everyone we knew and to choose Jesus anyway. Even more importantly, we had to then honestly grapple with the idea that if we were faced with that choice, we might make a different one—well, it's a lot to think about.

If anything, my life had mostly been better because of my relationship with Christ. The jobs I got as a teenager were because of people we knew at my Christian school. Heck, even after college, people would tell me how much they loved the Bible verse in my email signature. My decision to follow Jesus was never a hindrance to me in my life, but then again, why would it be? Christianity was a dominant force in the culture around me growing up. So when my church talked about persecution, it typically meant the way our values weren't exalted in every sector of our pluralistic society. We had come to expect acceptance and influence, and as "secular" values rose to the top, we would find ourselves on the outside. Criticism was the first step, and society's desire to hold space for multiple views threatened our cultural dominance, which made us feel persecuted because it made us uncomfortable.

How did your church growing up talk about persecution or cultural values? What examples, if any, did they use of your waning influence? How did they encourage you to view these interactions or push back against them? In my circles, if someone said, "Happy holidays" instead of "Merry Christmas," or if politicians failed to pass "pro-life" and "pro–traditional marriage" laws that reflected our beliefs, we saw it all as proof that Christians weren't just losing influence but would soon actively be persecuted.

I stopped thinking that way once I met people who experienced actual, deep persecution or who escaped it only because they had successfully lived a kind of double life to survive . . .

- The girl who taught Arabic at her family's mosque even though she follows Jesus

- The group of worshipers who were tracked and beaten by a group from the dominant religion in their region

- The prayer group that met in secret because religious meetings of any kind weren't allowed

- The family whose income dried up because now that they followed Christ no one would buy their goods, even if they needed them

- The man who was murdered because his neighbors didn't like that he was talking about Jesus

Persecution used to be a hypothetical or abstract concept for me. It was either cast as a future reality as we look toward the end of the world, or it was the notion that some people disagreeing with me was actually an affront to my rights and religion. But I couldn't think of it that way anymore. Not now that I had met people and heard stories that showed me what it looks like to be on the wrong end of harm done purely because of your religious beliefs. I couldn't stamp "persecution" at the top of anything that didn't follow my rules, and I certainly couldn't count it as a sign that we were near the end or that the church was truly threatened.

Christianity was born on the fringes. Hardship is one of the factors to consider when choosing to follow Christ, in the beginning and throughout Christian history. The experience of being the dominant religious culture was familiar to me but would be unfamiliar to many saints I would meet in America, around the world, and in the future kingdom come. Perhaps the white evangelical church experience I knew was threatened, but that is not the same as a threat to God or to all of Christianity. Looking back, thinking that the church could be threatened by losing power, that making space for other views meant mine was diminished, or that being criticized meant I was being persecuted seems immature, ignorant, and arrogant.

At some point I had to reckon with it all: What else was I confusing for persecution that was really just *life*? What did I believe was promised to me that may not quite be right? What could it really cost me to follow Jesus, and was I willing to pay that price? What does it look like to lay down your life when it's unlikely you'll actually have to do that?

The Ancient Expectation of Persecution

Jesus and the earliest believers didn't have the dominant religious culture experience that I did. When they spoke of persecution, it was not small, future, or abstract. They didn't have the power to make the rules, yet they strove to create a new society within their own. This kind of living, the kingdom kind, threatened the peace and status quo of not just the religious elite but also the Roman empire. Jesus knew what kind of toll that would take on their lived experiences. When we get to the end of the Beatitudes, which extols the virtues of the kingdom and prescribes the attitudes and actions of kingdom people, we see what we are to expect in return. And let me tell you, if this is the sales pitch, it's stunning that as many people jumped in as they did:

> Blessed are those who are persecuted for the sake of righteousness, for theirs is the kingdom of heaven. Blessed are you when people revile you and persecute you and utter all kinds of evil against you falsely on my account. Rejoice and be glad, for your reward is great in heaven, for in the same way they persecuted the prophets who were before you. (Matthew 5:10–12)

In these last few lines Jesus turns to describing how people will respond to disciples who live out the disruptive witness of the kingdom by defying the status quo. It is not a pleasant picture, but he adds a few notable caveats. Jesus knows that anyone who has a vested interest in keeping things as they are will fight back, but he is also careful to mention that not all pushback can be classified as persecution. He makes it clear at what point something falls under that umbrella: "For the sake of righteousness" and "on my account" are telltale signs of what makes something persecution. Persecution specifically refers to ill treatment for what is done in righteousness (or justice, because it's the same word, remember?) and for what is done on his account.

The whole of the Sermon on the Mount is painting for us a picture of what should be done on his account, and it has nothing to do with dominating culture. Rather, it is largely focused on how we position our hearts in order to break cycles that disrupt shalom and bring reconciliation to our relationships with those around us. It is the work of restoring shalom—peace, wholeness, integrity.[1] Notably missing from the list? Power or dominance.

Jesus then adds to this an important clause: "in the same way they persecuted the prophets who were before you." We think of prophets as important figures throughout the history of Israel because they make up a significant chunk of the Hebrew Bible, and that's not a wrong impression. They were important, but often they were considered more important in hindsight than they were in their day. Their job was to declare when and how Israel was in sin, and to call the people back to repentance or to suffer for it at the hands of the empires around them.

Spoiler alert: the prophets usually failed miserably at getting people to step back into God's way. According to tradition, many of them actually died because the people did not like what they heard and wanted to continue in rebellion.[2] The prophets spoke and lived to be a witness to the will of God for his people, and they were often struck down for that witness. Jesus is not just issuing a warning, he is painting a picture of who his people are to be in the world around them and the price they will probably pay for such disruption to those who seek to maintain the status quo of the time.

Living prophetically in the way of the kingdom means living a life of faithful disruption. It is seeing the layer of God's reality over every sphere of life and calling people to live into and up to that layer, but it often has consequences. In the upside-down values of the kingdom, the response to those consequences is not to fight back, but instead to witness by continuing to work for the good of all—even your persecutor—and to rejoice because you are following Christ even in your suffering and perhaps your death.

The Attitude When Facing Persecution

We don't have to go far to see the possible consequences of living in the way of Jesus. The book of Acts is filled with stories of violence and hardships faced by the earliest believers:

- Stephen is martyred

- Peter and John go to prison

- Paul encounters and escapes numerous death plots

- James, the brother of John, is killed

- Paul goes to prison

And this trend extends beyond the texts of the Bible and further into history. Paul and ten of the twelve original disciples were martyred, each one willingly going to their fate as they refused to stop walking the path Jesus had laid out for them, praising God the whole way. When reading early church literature, I was struck by how those Christians viewed their impending fates as they were marched across different countries in chains to be executed. They didn't see persecution and even certain death as a hindrance to their ability to be a disciple of Jesus. They saw it as the completion of their discipleship and as an opportunity to be a witness along the journey.

Ignatius of Antioch was a bishop of Antioch and an eventual martyr. During his time as a leader, the emperor Trajan issued a decree to worship the pagan gods. Ignatius was taken from his home and post in Antioch to Rome to meet wild beasts in an amphitheater.[3] He wrote several letters along the way, the last of which was written to churches in Rome. Back then, the letters became known as something of a "martyr's manual."[4] In all his words, he was not complaining about his chains or what waited for him in Rome. He wrote:

> For my part, I am writing to all the churches and assuring them that I am truly in earnest about dying for God—if only you yourselves put no obstacles in the way. I must implore you to do me no such untimely kindness; pray leave me to be a meal for the beasts, for it is they who can provide my way to God. I am His wheat, ground fine by the lions' teeth to be made purest bread for Christ. Better still, incite the creatures to become a sepulchre for me; let them not leave the smallest scrap of my flesh, so that I

need not be a burden to anyone after I fall asleep. When there is no trace of my body left for the world to see, then I shall truly be Jesus Christ's disciple.[5]

Catholic tradition holds that Ignatius heard the gospel from John the Apostle, and, being the third bishop of Antioch, he was likely ordained by Peter.[6] Instead of choosing a path of power, he chose a path of service to the church, even describing himself as a slave to it.

These early Christians were a disruptive force to the powerful. Even the title *Christian*—back then groups were often labeled by the leaders they followed—emphasized that they didn't see the Roman emperor as their ultimate authority, something the emperors of Rome did not appreciate.[7] More often than not, Christians found themselves at the mercy of those who made the rules and they took care of those whom the rules left behind.

But believers like Ignatius didn't aspire to rule. Later in his letter to the Romans, Ignatius writes, "To die in Jesus Christ is better than to be monarch of the widest bounds."[8] Those who found themselves in chains for the truth aspired to obey the one they followed with everything and, with their hope set firmly on the future, longed for union with Christ in death—completing their discipleship. They lived in light of the shalom promise of the gospel—a future where we are made complete and the world is whole again.

The Promise in Suffering

Have you ever heard of the idea of the "thought-terminating cliché"? It's the kind of phrase people use to shut down a conversation about something challenging, but in a way that is meant to sound nice. This happens sometimes in Christian circles when pain, suffering, or grief occur in someone's life. We don't always know what to say, so we want to comfort someone by giving their suffering a meaning. This comes out in phrases like

- God works in mysterious ways.

- Everything happens for a reason.

- All things work together for our good.

- If God brings you to it, he'll bring you through it.

- Well, the Bible says [insert any number of verses to make us feel good here].

These clichés tend to minimize someone's experience by framing their pain as in service of something bigger and better. If we admit their pain is senseless, we also must face the reality that something similar could happen to us one day. These clichés often serve the comforter rather than the sufferer, because it feels like offering something of value by pointing the sufferer back to God. But suffering of any kind is not usually alleviated with just a few trite words, and putting God's name on those pithy phrases doesn't make them more effective. The truth is that sometimes life sucks and suffering really hurts. It is inevitable. It's a part of being human, and worse, it's actually more or less promised to us believers if we're living in the countercultural way of Jesus and disrupting the status quo of the prevailing cultural, political, social, or economic paradigms.

It's true that the Bible also offers hope to the suffering, grieving, brokenhearted, persecuted, and martyred. But it's not an easy formula: "Suffer X amount and you can count on Y amount of joy and reward!" In all our suffering, whatever it looks like, still the promise is the same: God is near. God loves you. God will make all things right. Your reward is great in suffering because it is the reward of the redeemed and restored. It is the reward of Godself and being a part of the future world where everything has been set right again, but it is not always a reward we see break through in our suffering in this time and place.

Jesus' own life models this for us. As a man living on this earth, he experienced pain. His family lived for a time in exile in Egypt to keep him alive. He wasn't exactly well-received in every place by every group of people he encountered. Throughout his ministry there were plots to kill him. His cousin John is murdered for bearing the good news, and after his own arrest, Jesus is abandoned by his closest friends. All of this happens while he also knowingly marches toward the cross. He is put on trial, he is beaten, and he suffers immensely before he surrenders his spirit and dies. But in doing so, he made a way back to wholeness. To suffer for Christ is to share in the suffering of Christ and it is to have our joy completed when his glory is revealed (1 Peter 4:13). And his resurrection is our hope of resurrection too.

Though the goal of persecutors is to squash the spirit of the believers and with it the spread of the gospel message, the history of the church has proven the futility of this as well. After Pentecost, persecution begins in full force. Stephen becomes the first martyr as a pre-conversion Paul pushes to persecute this new sect in Jerusalem. He gets permission to drag people from their homes, and as he does so, the believers are pushed out into the world—taking the message of Jesus with them. He continues to chase them until he has his own experience on the road with Jesus. Then Paul becomes an object of the very persecution he'd spearheaded, eventually finding himself arrested. And as he faces trial after trial before important Roman leaders (including the emperor), Paul is writing letters, the church is growing, and the message of Jesus is going further and further out into the nations. The fire of faith the persecutors intended to quell only grew by igniting more hearts with the good news of Christ. God is not threatened. The church is not vanquished. Instead, suffering is all redeemed into our good and the good of others through our witness.

Our good is promised, but it doesn't mean we will see it today or that it will be proportional to our suffering during our time on earth before restoration. Our good is the goodness of God. Our good is resurrection and wholeness. Our good is the good of the world. And sometimes for living into that good, we suffer at the world's hand as Christ did.

Seeking the Peace

When I was young, I remember holding a tract in my hand with large bold letters at the top that read "Fire Insurance." It seemed clever and helpful to me then. I read it through and picked up phrases and ideas from it that I wanted to use to tell others about Jesus, because avoiding hell did seem like a top-tier benefit of becoming a Christian. With a few quick questions and affirmative answers, anyone could be saved a spot in heaven. I cringe a little now, because while I do believe that life in Christ means hell is not something we need to fear, we miss a crucial link in our discipleship when we make pain avoidance—even the eternal kind—the main thrust of the message. When we do that, we shortcut not just the cost of our discipleship but the point of our discipleship. We find this in the words of Jesus:

> Then Jesus told his disciples, "If anyone would come after me, let him deny himself and take up his cross and follow me. For whoever would save his life will lose it, but whoever loses his life for my sake will find it. For what will it profit a man if he gains the whole world and forfeits his soul? Or what shall a man give in return for his soul?" (Matthew 16:24–26 ESV)

Rome's way of keeping the peace was to kill those who made a fuss and had potential to upset the way things were. But shalom offers a stark contrast to this hollow peace of prosperity or complacency. It is a peace that comes through the self-sacrifice of individuals who are determined to obey the God who made the world and to participate with God in restoring it to the way it was always meant to be: whole, equal, abundant for everyone.

I was walking out of a church in Southeast Asia where persecution for following Christ was a possibility every day, and above the door hung a sign that read, "The more you suffer, the more you get blessing." It was green, unadorned, and the last thing people saw as they left a gathering to go into the world. It was a reminder to all who came and went that suffering was possible, but it wasn't the end. I think about that sign often.

I believe persecution and martyrdom are real—I've seen and heard too much to believe otherwise—but it's so easy to forget it here in the United States, where Christians' broad cultural dominance means we are often protected from what is a reality for so many believers around the world. I have been surprised over the years to find that while we are busy finding ways we believe the government or secular society are persecuting us, so much suffering and resistance to the spoken and lived message of the gospel comes from within the American evangelicalism I was a part of for most of my life.

When I was young, I was under the impression that the fight for the way of Jesus would happen between Christians and the world, but as I grew older and more familiar with the Scriptures myself, I found that most of the resistance I experienced when trying to live the way of Jesus was actually from those within the church itself. The call of Christ to take up the cross is to seek the wholeness of the kingdom, and in doing so, to know that not everyone will want the deeper peace it offers to us and to them, even if they are part of God's people. This becomes clear when churches or larger segments of Christianity call for unity when something opposed to the way of Jesus is happening within the church.

When we prioritize avoiding the hardship of repentance and reconciliation—often at the expense of those who are already marginalized—in order to preserve a reputation or a comfortable way of life, we settle for the hollow peace of the Roman empire and end up fighting against the goals of shalom. Those who choose to seek true peace then find themselves suffering and pushed to the outside at the hands of those inside the church. But if the call to take up our cross means anything, it means that walking through even this suffering can bring us closer to God. It can make us more complete disciples—individually and corporately—as we seek to be closer to his purposes.

Choosing to follow Jesus means choosing to walk the way he did—to be obedient to the will of God, to bring healing to people and communities, and to proclaim the gospel and the kingdom. That peace has a price, but we should not be afraid to pay it. Rather it is a risk we need to truly grapple with as we move through our lives and in our churches.

This is the cost of discipleship. Our success as disciples is not measured in our success on earth. Rather, it is in our choosing to follow Jesus every day, knowing the cost. It is not the hollow peace of avoiding hell or maintaining harmony. It is the complete peace of wholeness and restoration. That is our hope.

Meeting believers who actively experienced persecution helped me to realize that we must truly weigh the cost of our discipleship as a community, and we must be willing to pay it individually and collectively. I saw that perhaps we had become lax in our commitment to the way of Jesus and the people of God because we didn't have to take seriously the promise of threats and violence that come from the outside. And now as some of us are reexamining our relationship with American evangelical spaces, we struggle when we find a suffering we didn't expect that comes from those within that community.

Those of us only recently experiencing this hardship can especially learn from Black Americans and Christians, who have been marginalized and oppressed by white American Christians for centuries. Most white Christians will probably not face death for Christ or for any of our other defining characteristics, but we will likely suffer at the hands of those who prefer to fight for the status quo or their own comfort. We can learn how to process our pain well from those who have experienced it in their communities. These threats are real and present for them, and they have been grappled with for centuries. Eminent theologian James Cone writes this about what the lynching tree can teach us about the cross from the lynching era in America (at its worst from 1880 to 1940):

> In that era, the lynching tree joined the cross as the most emotionally charged symbols in the African American community—symbols that represented both death and the promise of redemption, judgment and the offer of mercy, suffering and the power of hope. Both the cross and the lynching tree represented the worst in human beings and at the same time 'an unquenchable ontological thirst' for life that refuses to let the worst determine our final meaning.[9]

In the cross, we see the best and worst of humanity and the human experience. The worst is in the suffering inflicted upon the innocent at the hands of those who want hollow peace that oppresses, and the best is in the hope of redemption contained on the other side of the cross that was obtained by our Savior. The pursuit of reconciliation and peace that we seek in our churches and in the world comes at a cost, a deeply painful one. But the pain inflicted on us by others does not determine the meaning of our lives. Christ determines our meaning, and he is near to us in our pain because he, too, has suffered. Like Christ, we suffer with the sure hope of resurrection on the horizon. And it's because of resurrection that I dare to believe that my past pain isn't the end and that the church can be transformed into a space of joyful practice for us all.

Part Two

JOURNEY INTO JOYFUL PRACTICE

EIGHT

Compelled by Compassion

IT LOOKED LIKE someone had put trees on the moon. The landscape was dusty brown, covered in a haze of sand that blew around us. The sun blazed down on us as we looked out across the cratered plain. This part of East Africa was flat, but we could see hills in the distance. Otherwise, nothing but a few trees sparsely dotted the view before us.

We had just driven for what seemed like hours on a road so bumpy that most actually drove in the ruts now worn down beside the asphalt because it was smoother there. When we finally parked and looked around, it looked exactly like you might picture the middle of nowhere: dusty and empty with the sun's rays beaming directly on our skin. A large tree stood in front of us, and a group of people was gathering there.

We walked our way up to the tree to stand in its shade. It was here that I first encountered the legacy of Brian. Under this tree, my party and I worshiped alongside three other small church groups who had gathered here. It was unusual for them to do so, as they typically worship in their own areas, but they came together this one time while we were in town. It was beautiful. The people gathered were clearly from different tribes or traditions, wearing a variety of brightly colored outfits. They sang with us, danced for us, and listened alongside us as we heard Brian give a sermon. When it was time to give an offering, they didn't just put money in a plate. They gave crops, brooms, money, and other items that they possessed. We praised God for it all.

Later that day, I got to sit with a few people to talk with Brian. His friend had introduced him to Jesus when he lived elsewhere. He was ravenous for the truth, and he took in all the training he could find. One day he visited the small town where he grew up, and when he saw the people, his heart was filled with love for them. He knew he needed to come back here to share Christ. So, he did. He packed up his family and they moved their lives.

Brian was an evangelist, sure, but he was more than that. He was a pastor, a mentor, a caretaker of bodies and souls. It was his compassion that drove him. Every place he went in the area, he saw the needs of the people, and he would spend his days getting grants for them, finding partnerships to get food and water to them, and then preaching the gospel. It wasn't just about their eternal lives, it was about their "here and now."

He logged long days, with lots of miles on a motorcycle to make it to the remote areas where people lived and many hours spent with people giving them what they needed. But Brian didn't resent any of the people or regret any of the hours or miles. His eyes would fill with tears when he spoke of the people he served because he loved them so much.

It's beautiful when you see that love for the flock reflected in the eyes of the shepherd, but it also goes horribly wrong when something else takes the place of that love. We've witnessed it here in the United States: The pastors who trade prayers and promises for money from those who listen to them. The leaders who leverage their power to create systems that give them opportunity to commit and to hide heinous acts of sexual abuse. The church discipline processes that protect reputations of the church and its leaders but not the congregants who may be suffering within it. These have become stories we're all too familiar with in recent days.

I find it hard some days to believe Christian institutions can be worth staying in and fighting for, but I still believe that the church is a force for good—for those within it and for the world around it. But we've lost our way in practice. In this section of the book, we're taking a new journey, one into the joyful practice of our faith. We'll wind our way through this leg of the trip with our eyes on reorienting how we think about and do the work of the church. What better place to start than the top?

Redefining Power

One of my favorite traits of Jesus is his way of calmly subverting expectations and turning everything upside down. The way he modeled leadership was no different. In the gospel of Mark, it seems like the author goes out of his way to actually show how different Jesus is from other leaders.

The other leaders are oppressors and gatekeepers. They're trying to keep everyone in their place and to take advantage of their current status to leverage more money or status or power.

Jesus shakes up all the rules, and it makes them very uncomfortable. So uncomfortable they don't want him around anymore. Mark uses his two feeding narratives (yep, he has two) to make this point. The first subtly compares Jesus to Herod, the second to the religious rulers. The reasons vary, but the outcome is the same. They shut out and take advantage of the very people Jesus includes, and he doesn't just include them, he cares for them.

Taking Advantage and Saving Face (Mark 6:7–44)

There aren't a lot of flashbacks in Scripture, but Mark 6 has one of the most famous examples. After Jesus sends the disciples out on a mission and while they're traveling out to the wilderness, we get a flashback sequence to the death of John the Baptist (Mark 6:14–29). This is surprising because it's out of sequence. It simply doesn't belong at this point in this narrative. So we have to ask why. When stories are interspersed in unusual ways, there is often intention in that. Grouped together, stories can point to a theme we ought to pick up on. This story feels out of place, but that's what helps us know it's right where it should be. When you dig into the stories, you see they are parallel in a few ways—there are guests, food, and a leader there to provide. And in seeing how Herod hosts his guests and how Jesus creates a table in the wilderness for those he didn't even want to be there, we see a contrast of leadership style and values.

Herod Antipas was one of the sons of Herod the Great. As an aristocratic Jew, he had roots in the nation, but as the governor of Judea and Perea, where Galilee is located, he also wielded the authority of the Roman Empire.[1] As part of the ruling class, it is likely that many of the collective resources of the nation flowed to Herod and the city centers on its way to Rome. This gave Herod increased wealth and separated him from those on the margins from whom part of his wealth came.[2] Herod makes only one appearance in Mark, but he leaves his mark, along with other representatives of the Roman government throughout the gospel.

This story in Mark 6 shares the details of his infamous birthday banquet that results in the death of John the Baptist. It sounds like quite the party. Food, entertainment, and the best of the best right there. The details of the narrative reveal Herod's priorities. First, Mark tells us about the guest list, full of the who's who of the elite—military commanders, high officials, and leaders in Galilee. Then we see how Herod uses the resources that he gained from the people of the kingdom. He feeds and entertains his guests lavishly, and when he finds the entertainment of his daughter's dance to be more than satisfactory for them all, he makes a promise for her to have anything up to half his kingdom.

Mind you, Herod doesn't have the authority to give half his kingdom. His kingdom actually belongs to Rome. He's essentially an aristocratic steward who gets to skim off the top. But hey, bragging rights, right? In the end, his daughter asks for John the Baptist's head, which is a shame. He likes John, but now he's faced with a decision. Save face or do what's right? His final priority is revealed. He decides to capitulate to his daughter's request to have John the Baptist murdered, a result of his wife's vendetta. One last platter is prepared for him and his guests . . . the one that contains John's head.

Herod is used by those with a grudge to take the life of an innocent man, a theme that will recur later in Mark's story with our main character. But we clearly see what Herod's priorities are. He will do what it takes to maintain and elevate his status, even at the expense of the innocent.

I don't know about you, but I couldn't help but think of the many recent Christian scandals and crises. These revealed to us just how many leaders were protected—at the expense of the victims—for the sake of the church's or organization's reputation because they were showing so much "fruit" in terms of growth numbers or dollars raised. For example, one pastor, known for his brash style, resigned from leadership only after numerous confrontations with church elders.[3] Another international leader passed away in 2020 and after his death, it was revealed that he was guilty of sexual misconduct and abuse, and many in his organization knew and protected his reputation.[4] And in 2019, the *Houston Chronicle* revealed the extent of sexual abuse that took place in the Southern Baptist Convention and the ways those crimes were mishandled by the churches and their leadership.[5] These failures in leadership mirror Herod's failure. Save face, not the victims.

But Jesus is the opposite.

After John's death, Mark turns the story's focus back on Jesus. Though he wanted to be alone with his disciples, as he arrives into the wilderness, he finds a crowd from villages around waiting for him. If it were me, I would have run away. The introvert in me would have circled back to that boat in an instant, but Jesus takes it all in stride. Unlike Herod's invited guests of high stature in the community, Jesus' guests have no names or titles. They're not even on the guest list, but the text says, "He had compassion on them, because they were like sheep without a shepherd" (6:34). And here's where we start to see the contrast in Herod's and Jesus' priorities.

Instead of entertaining people, Jesus taught them. Instead of taking from the innocent to give to those of high standing, he gathers the common resources in order to multiply them for all those in attendance (who have likely suffered from the empire's policies). Then he feeds people physically just as he has done spiritually. In the end, though he had no worldly authority of the empire behind him, Jesus showed he had authority from God to feed mankind spiritually and physically. In this way, he demonstrated the priorities of the kingdom of God to five thousand "little people"—hospitality, truth, compassion, and care—and he did so as one with authority from God, showing himself as a compassionate King.

Gatekeeping (Mark 7–8)

Imperial powers aren't the only ones Jesus is held up next to. Brace yourselves, because he's also contrasted with the religious leaders and how they wield their power. When we move beyond the first feeding narrative, we see Jesus going toe-to-toe with the Pharisees.

In the days of Jesus, there were a few distinct classes of religious leaders. Pharisees and Sadducees are the two we encounter most in the New Testament, along with others known only as scribes and elders. The Pharisees were largely associated with the ritual practices in the Jerusalem temple. Their name likely comes from a term related to "separation," especially with regard to separating from impure food and from eating with those who didn't keep strictly to purity and tithing laws.[6]

The gospel narratives are part of a tradition of literature that often focused on speaking against Pharisees in the time the narratives were written, rather than the time they were written about. It is important to keep that distinction in mind, because it's likely that the gospel writers are reacting to the resistance against Christianity as it was emerging while they were writing rather than resistance during the life of Jesus. The Pharisees are characterized as legalistic, but without adhering to their own strict rules. In other words, they're often the hypocrites in the stories. It's important to note that the teachings of Jesus even reflect some Pharisaic ethics.[7] So when we get to narratives like these, we need to be careful to see the Pharisees as characters or placeholders for a particular kind of person, rather than read these stories as a historically accurate portrayal of their tradition or actions at the time. Thinking that way has led to Christians excusing harmful behavior against Jews throughout history. Here I will use the word "Pharisees" for ease of communication because it's what is used in the text, but what I mean is the kind of hypocritical legalist that they represent in the story, though they were not like that in history.

Prior to this section of the gospel narrative, Jesus has a few run-ins with the Pharisees that involve the cleanliness of a newly healed leper and keeping the Sabbath. It was these encounters that actually prompted these characters to partner with the Herodians to plot to kill Jesus in the story.

When we get to Mark 7:1–23, the disciples are breaking the rules about ritual cleanliness before meals, and the Pharisees are not happy. They confront Jesus about it, asking why he doesn't hold his own people to the law, and throughout the discourse, we see the priorities of these leaders revealed as Jesus confronts them.

First, we see they value the outward appearance of cleanliness, which Jesus flips by declaring that it is not what goes in but what comes out that defiles. Second, we see them upholding laws that separate Jews from Gentiles. Jesus changes this standard by declaring all foods clean. Third, they uphold these restrictions as the "tradition of the elders," which in some cases created conflicts that did not keep with the original intent of the Torah laws. All of these resulted in the characters under the label "Pharisees" creating classes of insiders and outsiders, according to rules of ritual purity. They're looking at the outside, and our Jesus, well, he changes the narrative.

In the end, Jesus shows that the way of God is more concerned with internal purity than external, which paves the way for a ministry that opens the door to a new group of people, the Gentiles.

What I love about Mark is that now, he shows Jesus walking his talk. After this spat with the Pharisee characters, the whole crew packs up and journeys into Gentile lands. His first stop is Tyre, a place that was not only Gentile but also likely hostile to Jews. Much like he did in his ministry in Jewish territory, Jesus performs an exorcism for the Syrophoenician woman's daughter (Mark 7:24–30). Then he moves on to heal a man who is deaf (7:31–37) before he finds himself once more in the wilderness (8:1–10)—this time in Gentile territory. The echoes of the previous feeding narrative are strong. The stories are very similar, and Jesus is caring for the outsiders just like he did the insiders a chapter earlier.

Now we're in the wilderness with a crowd of four thousand Gentiles. Similar to the disciples, whom the Pharisees had witnessed eating a meal with Jesus earlier, this crowd has been with Jesus for a while. This time the people with Jesus are not bound by any ritualistic rules. By contrast, they would not be expected or perhaps even allowed to engage in the rituals of Judaism due to their heritage. Yet, like the feeding of five thousand Jewish men and others in another wilderness, Jesus extends the same compassion to these Gentiles. He gathers their present resources, and he performs the same miracle with the same steps. Thus, he subverted expectations and opened a door for Gentiles to be welcomed with the same hospitality, truth, compassion, and care into the kingdom of God.

There are no longer separations or rigid rules that keep them from the presence of God. Jesus uses his spiritual authority to change the rules and show himself a benevolent Lord in addition to King.

"Beware of the Yeast"

This section of Mark's Gospel ends with an admonition from Jesus: "Beware of the yeast of the Pharisees and the yeast of Herod" (8:15). Yeast is an interesting substance. My husband brews beer, and we also make wine together on occasion. We're a little familiar with yeast. It's the magical ingredient that turns what we jokingly call "bread tea," the water from the malted grains, into beer. It's the fermenting agent. You don't need a lot of it. In fact, for about five gallons of beer, you only need to add about an ounce of yeast. But even that little amount transforms the entire batch. Adding particular yeasts creates the desired flavors or style of beer, but on occasion, wild yeast gets in there. Did you know that yeast is almost everywhere? I didn't. But it is. If the wrong yeast or another contaminant that doesn't play nice with yeast gets introduced, it can "infect" the beer. Wild yeast produces the wrong flavors and can ruin the whole batch. When a batch gets infected, it cannot be saved. The entire batch must be thrown out.

When Jesus brings up the yeast of these two groups, we see that it's not the kind of yeast that will transform the world into the kingdom of God. The contrasts are written throughout the rest of this gospel account. We see the effects of this yeast:

- When Jesus flips over the money changing tables, he interrupts two things—the flow of money and the flow of sacrifice in the corrupted systems (Mark 11:15–19).

- Jesus talks about money, answering questions about taxes (Mark 12:13–17) and pointing out the widow who gave from her poverty (Mark 12:41–44). All of this lies against the backdrop of Herod and the religious leaders in the temple who misuse the resources, who seek status from the money collected.

- Herodians and religious leaders conspire to get Jesus arrested, and he goes on trial before the Jewish council (Mark 14:53–65) and the Roman governor (Mark 15:1–15).

Mark paints an ominous picture. When we seek power, status, and money, we can probably find it, but making that pursuit our purpose might also keep us from seeing the goodness of God and pointing other people to him. We might even be willing to sacrifice those who call out our misuse of power and resources in order to keep them intact. It's not about the resources themselves, it's about the motivation and stewardship of them. The wild yeast of motivation for celebrity can lead to the corruption of the whole batch—abuse and misuse of the people one leads and the resources they give.

The Good Yeast

It is easy to lose track of our priorities by focusing on maintaining status, attaining wealth at the expense of others—even if unknowingly—and keeping up external appearances. When I look around at the leaders that have failed us, I see people who were talented, charismatic, and capable of so much good. I even see that they did so much good, but somewhere the wrong yeast got in. Their hearts got infected, and what was once a ministry of good became driven by power or other sinister aims. Some of them know it, some of them don't.

But Jesus showed us the way of the kingdom of God. As both King and Lord, he focused on the priorities of heaven on earth. Driven by compassion, he fed people spiritually, and he took care of them physically. Jesus showed us how to care for each other in a world that asks us to care for ourselves, and that is the essence of leadership.

It makes me think of Brian in East Africa. He gave up the life he knew for the one he was called to by his compassion. He spends days and weeks not to elevate himself nor consolidate his power. Instead, he trains others to lead in their areas so they can multiply the work without him. He checks in on them, loves them, holds them accountable, and he has people like that for himself too.

We don't need higher platforms for our leaders. Platforms isolate leaders from those they're meant to serve and from those who can check their hearts. At some point, the whole enterprise often shifts to preserving the platform instead of caring for the people. Jesus wasn't like that. Jesus was with the people. He saw their needs. In fact, my hunch is that Jesus was probably hungry too. He was human, after all. He noticed the need they all shared, and he worked with them and with God to meet that need. The people were empowered through sharing their resources, and God multiplied them.

I think we can learn from that. Instead of building bigger stages, let's build more tables. More intimate circles to remind us that we all need the love of God, the care of our neighbors, and the rooting out of sin in our lives. These stories in Mark remind us that Jesus taught, and then he grouped the people together to break bread with one another as he provided for them. Maybe if we had tables instead of platforms, we'd remember how God used meager offerings of bread to feed the crowd. Maybe we'd remember that's our offering too.

Brian was a table-builder. He didn't think about how he could be above the people. He instead continually strove to be with the people. Leaders who do not connect with those they lead also do not know what their people need. The table equalizes us. It keeps us together, talking, and taking care of one another.

Lately, I've stopped just following the leaders everyone else is following—the ones with fancy words and big personalities, and I've started looking for the lesser known, deeply devoted, and continually faithful ones that are quietly serving in their corner of the world. We need more leaders like those, and it starts with us asking more from their character than from their charisma. We need leaders who want to be with us and not above us. We need to follow them, and we need to become them. With leaders like these we start to see that we, too, have the capacity to love and to lead this way, the way Jesus loved and led. Perhaps then compassion would compel us to bring the whole gospel to each other and the world because we felt that together we had the resources to do that and a Savior who modeled the way.

NINE

Confidence in the Spirit

IT WAS SO dark that we needed the headlights from the SUV we were driving through rural East Africa to light the way to the front door of the church building. We stepped carefully through the door since there was no light inside either. Our role there was twofold—some would stay to encourage the local churches, and others of us were there to document the work and stories. We were late, and they had been waiting all day. Though we expected frustration, we were met with warm hellos and welcomes. We smiled and met with everyone, but I had to splinter off to meet with a few of the leaders.

While we went to a local church member's home, the rest of the East African group in the church was eagerly waiting to hear from the other Americans in our little traveling party. I heard about it later. After a couple of my travel companions shared something from Scripture, eyes turned to my husband, who loves Jesus but does not consider himself a teacher, preacher, or pastor, and definitely did not come to speak in front of a crowd who expected him to be one of those. Though he was caught off guard, he had a word to offer.

He pulled up the Bible app on his phone and read from 2 Timothy 4:13, "When you come, bring the cloak that I left with Carpus at Troas, also the books, and above all the parchments." He went on to explain that he likes this verse because it offers a picture of Paul's imperfect humanity. It shows he was just like us—he even forgot his cloak sometimes—and if Paul could be like us and also be a great teacher and evangelist, then maybe there was hope for us too. When I rejoined the group, all I heard were rave reviews of his speaking. The churches there were entirely led by laypeople, and those laypeople had been trained by other laypeople. There weren't fancy degrees from Bible colleges and seminaries, nor were there titles like reverend, bishop, or apostle. It turns out that what they needed to hear was that all of us are capable of being at least a little like Paul, and that he was more like us than perhaps we thought.

In that church in East Africa and many others in different locations, I noticed that the power wasn't concentrated in the hands of the few but the many. There were leaders of movements—the ones who had been trained or supported in sharing the gospel and planting churches in new towns across the country—but they were guides for the smaller churches under their care, not necessarily authority figures. They nurtured relationships and dynamics within the church bodies so that others would have the knowledge and skills to keep the church going when the leaders left.

The weekly meetings and everyday ministries were run not by the few but the many, each using their gifts to contribute to the worship and care of the community. Someone who had a guitar or djembe would lead music. Someone who saw something new in Scripture that week would share what they learned with everyone else. Someone who saw their neighbor in need would suggest prayers and practical ways of meeting that need to the group. The hierarchy was flat. Everyone knew they had a role to play in the life of the church, and they were expected and empowered to do that.

At first, I remember being a little shocked. Where I came from, worship gatherings highlighted only a few key faces, and they were the ones with official titles like pastor or minister. My church life had a hierarchy oriented around officials and highly educated leaders. It wasn't like that here. Everyone sat in a circle, and I was used to only a few standing on the stage.

Who will make sure the church is taught all the right doctrines? Who will show them what to do? Who will make sure they don't stray from the way of Jesus? For a head-centered person like me, these questions can be difficult. I have spent most of my life in search of the right answers and clearly marked boundaries in order to make sure I was always in the correct camp. I read books, listened to pastors from all over the United States, and even had some formal theological training. But what do you do when you do not have access to those resources? Who is a qualified minister when there's no one official to formally train or ordain? What if we each have a role to play in the church, and not just a few of us?

Spiritual Authority

I've learned a lot of life and leadership lessons from cheer-leading. For many years, I was a cheerleader, cheerleading coach, and choreographer. At one time, I had a business where I coached cheerleading coaches, because there were so many of them who had been handed a cheerleading program at their school but had zero previous experience. What I discovered was that the easy part was teaching them the skills of the sport, and a lot of that was because they had done the hard part already. They said yes to the role, they wore their authority humbly, and they cared about the members of their team. That's what makes a good leader in any sphere of life— care and character. If you've got the heart, the rest will follow because you're committed to the people. I think we see this same kind of order play out in Scripture too.

By typical American definitions, the members of most churches I've been in overseas would not be qualified to lead. They did not have extensive theological training like we expect of pastors and ministers, and some of them had been Christians for a very short time. The churches weren't structured to rely on those who had been formally trained. They relied on those who had been transformed by following Jesus. In a way, this was the same kind of work the early church had to do.

When the church was beginning, the New Testament didn't exist—and what we now regard as Scripture was still being written and hadn't even been canonized into the collection of books we now call the Christian Bible. People with little training and little guidance in Christian doctrine and practices had to figure out what it looks like to live and worship together as the community of God. That's part of why we have a New Testament at all. The letters and stories we read there were early Christians working out their theology and sharing their best practices in real time. Those who experienced life with Christ physically were tasked with passing on what they knew so more could experience this way of life. We see this in Paul's writings. He even spells it out to Timothy: "And what you have heard from me through many witnesses entrust to faithful people who will be able to teach others as well" (2 Timothy 2:2).

The strategy is clear: those of us who do have resources must find the faithful who don't and pass on what we believe and practice. Theological training doesn't have to be formal to be effective, but even more importantly, faithfulness does not require formality. What Paul considered to be faithful also wasn't equated to having extensive knowledge and experience. This can be seen in the various requirements he gives for elders in 1 Timothy 3: faithful in marriage, not quarrelsome, self-controlled, temperate, respectable, hospitable, not violent, a good reputation with outsiders, and the list goes on. While "able to teach" is among them, it does not carry with it the requirement or ideal of formal training. The requirements are about who the elders are, not how much they know. Somehow Paul trusted that in the absence of his presence and eventually the absence of Timothy's presence, the faith would remain on track in the hands of the Spirit-filled faithful who would pass it on.

One of my favorite Bible stories illustrates this well. In Acts 8, we see Philip ministering in Samaria. Suddenly, he is called away by the Spirit and meets an Ethiopian eunuch along the way. The eunuch is eager to understand a passage from Isaiah. When Philip comes upon him, at the prompting of the Spirit he sits with him and explains everything. Where the Spirit made the way, it also made the opportunity. The eunuch that day chooses to believe and be baptized in the next water they see.

That's usually where the story stops. It's read as a celebration of belief and a believer's baptism, and we don't often talk about what comes next: "When they came up out of the water, the Spirit of the Lord snatched Philip away; *the eunuch saw him no more* and went on his way rejoicing" (Acts 8:39, emphasis added). Belief, baptism, and bye-bye. Philip is gone, and the eunuch goes on to his home rejoicing and taking the gospel with him. But did you notice what is missing? There are no long discourses on how to run a church or the right way to believe and behave. Nope, the eunuch goes on home so the gospel can take shape in a contextualized way. Willie James Jennings in his commentary on Acts puts it this way:

> The Spirit has intervened, and that intervention was also redemptive. The eunuch is not left alone. He is left free in his joy. Disciples do need direction and guides, but first disciples must know their freedom in Jesus Christ. The church has often been too impatient and sometimes downright fearful of that freedom, choosing instead to quickly impose an image of the true, the good, and the beautiful example on those who have been made free by the Spirit. God would have none of this for the Ethiopian. There will be no correct or proper image of a disciple, no bodily model by which to pattern himself, and no one to begin a process of erasure or eradication of his differences. Philip will not be allowed to stay to tell him who to be or how to be, how to see himself or receive a preloaded life script in Christ.[1]

The eunuch had the same Scriptures as the early church—he was reading Isaiah. He didn't get any extra training or catechesis in all the exact right Christian doctrines. After his baptism, he walked away transformed by Christ, guided by the Holy Spirit, and shaped by the story of the God of Israel as he went off to begin to form a new culture of the church in a new place. And like the eunuch, we, too, can have confidence in that freedom we have experienced through our encounters with God to form us into the disciple we are meant to become.

Spiritual Ability

Back when I would choreograph cheerleading routines for teams across the country, one thing I could always count on is that every team will have a spectrum of talent, and yet, when they're planning on going to competition, every team must meet the requirements on the scoresheet. Most of the time, there is a way to feature your star athletes that also allows the rest of the team to shine, but one area where this can get hairy is when it comes to stunts. When putting stunt sequences together, there are two philosophies to maximizing your score. The first is to heavily feature the skills of a few star athletes by putting them all in one group and letting the other groups be the "backup singers," if you will. The second is to equalize the groups so that you can have strong and synchronized groups across the board. I'm a big believer in the second philosophy, because it gives the stronger athletes a chance to help others who need help, and it makes each group a part of the whole. Everyone contributes in their own way, and when we work together as a team, we are able to do more than we thought we could. I think that's how the church should work too.

We can have confidence that the same Holy Spirit who dwells in church leaders, Paul, the apostles, the eunuch, and the person who sits next to you in church dwells in each of us. Though the way the Spirit shows up in each of us will be different, it doesn't mean that one kind of gift or manifestation of the Spirit is needed more than another:

> Now there are varieties of gifts but the same Spirit, and there are varieties of services but the same Lord, and there are varieties of activities, but it is the same God who activates all of them in everyone. To each is given the manifestation of the Spirit for the common good. . . . All these are activated by one and the same Spirit, who allots to each one individually just as the Spirit chooses. (1 Corinthians 12:4–7, 11)

When the Spirit came at Pentecost, it did not come more or less to any one person. Everyone who believed received, and each one also inherited the responsibility to use their gifts and pass on their faith. This is our inherent spiritual authority promised in Acts 1:8, "But you will receive power when the Holy Spirit has come upon you, and you will be my witnesses in Jerusalem, in all Judea and Samaria, and to the ends of the earth." This promise belongs to all of us in Christ, and it is Christ who shows us how to use it:

> So Jesus called them and said to them, "You know that among the Gentiles those whom they recognize as their rulers lord it over them, and their great ones are tyrants over them. But it is not so among you; instead, whoever wishes to become great among you must be your servant, and

whoever wishes to be first among you must be slave of all.
For the Son of Man came not to be served but to serve,
and to give his life a ransom for many." (Mark 10:42–45)

The power we receive is not one of earthly power structures and seats of domination. It is not an authority that over-
powers. It is an authority that empowers. It does not rule. It
serves. And as the great commission makes clear, it is an
authority used for making disciples—baptizing and teaching
to obey, and therefore, embody witness in the world. That is
the purpose for which we are empowered.

When we emphasize teaching and talent in our churches,
we can tend to outsource discipleship to the few. We become
known by the famous people we follow because they seem
to have it figured out. The Corinthians had this tendency,
too—claiming to be of Paul or of Apollos. This desire to be
following the star (or even to be the star) of the team was
a sign of their immaturity, because they failed to recognize
that God does the work through the leaders and that God
wants to do the work through us too.[2] The Spirit gave each
of us our specific gifts to care for and shape one another as
a witness to Christ, because we are all disciples not of our
leaders but of Christ himself. Rather than be known only by
our leaders, we should be known for how the Spirit moves
each of us to contribute to our communities. We don't need
to hide because our gifts seem small or unimportant.

Likewise, we shouldn't seek to lead because we want to
be in charge or dominate the conversation. Instead we can
come together humbly knowing that we need each other
to live fully and love well.[3] We not only each have authority because of the Spirit, but we each have responsibility

because of the Spirit. Discipleship is the responsibility of all of us, not the few with lots of training and talent. There is no spiritual hierarchy. Perhaps we appoint leaders to guide us along the way, but they are not the ones responsible for the disciples we become or make. That is on all of us. But more than that, we are all equipped uniquely, and our contributions make the body of Christ stronger.

It takes all of us to be faithful witnesses. It takes a community working together to meet the needs of those inside and outside the church and to create the guardrails that keep us focused on our purpose while maintaining our integrity. Together, the body of Christ can and should work effectively for the common good. It starts with each of us owning our role in that responsibility, and letting the Spirit work through our willingness. One of my greatest joys is to watch someone thrive in their gifts and others grow because of it. I love knowing who to call or connect when something comes up that is in their wheelhouse. Acting as the body of Christ doesn't just allow us to do more better, but it also allows us to do it together—which is a lot more fun.

TEN

Heads, Hands, and Hearts of Christ

I WAS STARTING to forget just how cold I was. Our trip had taken us from extreme heat to near freezing temperatures as we traversed from one country into another. I hadn't packed the layers I needed now, and it probably didn't help that my shoes were in a neat line outside the door of this one-room apartment, along with everyone else's. So with a shiver, I sat on the cold concrete floor and crossed my arms, hoping to keep a little more heat in my body. "Apartment" might make you think it was bigger than it was. It was a room with a bed, a hotplate, a chair, and a closet. But today, this room was a church. As we began our time of worship together, the voices in the room began to sing together in beautiful harmony. Suddenly I wasn't worried about the cold anymore.

175

I just wanted to be there, in that moment, worshiping with every part of me—body, mind, soul.

But doing that is a challenge when you don't speak the same language or have the same customs. I kept looking around at the faces of the men and women sitting in a circle on this cold floor. Each face was full of joy and reverence. They hadn't known our God long, but I got the feeling that they knew God well. As they sang, a woman from the neighborhood came to the door and peeked her head in. The members of the church finished their song, welcomed her, and invited her in. She was smiling, and as she came to find a place in the circle, she said, "I saw the shoes outside your door, and I knew you must be meeting for church now. I have come to be saved." I was flabbergasted. For all my years in the faith, I am not sure I have ever heard someone state a desire to be saved as plainly as that without any prompting. And right there, in that room, in that moment, she was. She committed to follow Jesus. It was shocking and beautiful, but it didn't happen by accident.

That moment happened because of the people in that room. Not just their regular corporate worship that she recognized by the collection of shoes outside the door, but also the witness of each one as they lived their lives in that community. I had almost a week with those believers, but in that short time I learned a lot about what it means to live as the community of Christ in the world—what it truly looks like to be disciples who are transformed and who transform.

When the woman showed up at the door, she didn't talk about all the information they had given her, though I don't doubt they shared the message of the gospel with words as well as their lives. She hadn't been handed a tract or pamphlet. She had been watching their actions and their lives. They weren't just good speakers or debaters. They were good humans. The fruit of their discipleship showed us as much.

I wish I could say every interaction with someone who follows Jesus I have had in my life had that same air about it. I doubt others could say that about every interaction they've had with me. But in a time when so many aspects of my faith were shifting or had shifted, I encountered more than one Christian who decided I wasn't good enough because those shifts made them uncomfortable. I might ask a question or share a doubt and be met with blank stares, stern warnings, simplistic platitudes, or all-out hostility.

Like a lot of the people that have dropped by and hurled hurtful words my way, I was taught a definition of discipleship that had been reduced to successful retention of Bible knowledge, certainty in a particular subset of beliefs, and enthusiastic policing of those beliefs in personal and public spaces. The success story in that context is a person who has a lot of knowledge, who could draw the biggest crowd, or who kept all the right rules. And, believe me, I get the temptation to that way of thinking, because it is so much easier to measure what people know and what people do. Don't get me wrong—those are important. Jesus often talked about how if we are part of his people then we will do particular things. But it strikes me that so often in the Bible, the main measures for success as disciples are actually laid out in messy terms. They're qualitative instead of quantitative, and they require more than just believing and behaving. They require becoming too. And maybe that means all the quantitative ways we measure being disciples don't quite capture the whole picture, either.

Not of Human Credentials

I try to keep all this under wraps, but I'm going to let you in on a little secret. The truth is—and this is hard to say—I am an achiever. Deep down in my bones, I love to rack up awards and degrees and certifications and words of affirmation. I think this may be a side effect of my Enneagram 5 tendency to need to be an expert, and, despite all my study, never feeling like one. Because the thing is: the more you know, the more you know that you don't know. It's a vicious cycle, and even knowing this, I often persist—chasing another credential to make sure I am competent and ready to take on whatever comes my way. Unfortunately, what you realize eventually when following Jesus is that no human credential does really stack up. Paul lays it all out in Philippians 3:4b–9:

> If anyone else has reason to be confident in the flesh, I have more: circumcised on the eighth day, a member of the people of Israel, of the tribe of Benjamin, a Hebrew born of Hebrews; as to the law, a Pharisee; as to zeal, a persecutor of the church; as to righteousness under the law, blameless.
>
> Yet whatever gains I had, these I have come to regard as loss because of Christ. More than that, I regard everything as loss because of the surpassing value of knowing Christ Jesus my Lord. For his sake I have suffered the loss of all things, and I regard them as rubbish, in order that I may gain Christ and be found in him, not having a righteousness of my own that comes from the law but one that comes through faith in Christ, the righteousness from God based on faith.

Paul's résumé was stacked. He was at the head of the class in all the Jewish markers of righteousness. He didn't just follow the rules, he had the titles and responsibilities to back it all up. And yet, it was not enough. He considered it loss, rubbish, *dung* compared to knowing Christ. It was not on this basis that he was a disciple, let alone a *good* one. It was not on this basis that he was counted righteous or grew spiritually. His roles and years of study and rising in the ranks did not matter for him, and it does not matter for us either. A person can be a pastor, a well-known scholar, and respected leader, and yet miss the mark. We can stack up our credentials as much as we'd like, but they will not count toward our discipleship. As Paul reminds us here, only the faithfulness of Christ and our lived imitation of his life matter.

Not about Checking Boxes

Just like I am good with pursuing credentials, I am also excellent at checking boxes. I am a rule follower and a doer of the right things. Any measure of productivity and faithful living you can throw at me, you better believe I am striving for ways to check every last task off that list.

The bad news (though these days I see it as good news) is that Jesus kind of upends that whole paradigm. We see this come up in Galatians. Paul is focused on explaining to the church full of Gentiles why they don't need to worry about circumcision and following the law of the Jews. Some teachers are telling them that they need to do it all, but Paul argues for living in the freedom of Christ's grace and being aligned with the incoming new creation kingdom:

> By contrast, the fruit of the Spirit is love, joy, peace, patience, kindness, generosity, faithfulness, gentleness, and self-control. There is no law against such things. And

those who belong to Christ have crucified the flesh with its passions and desires. If we live by the Spirit, let us also be guided by the Spirit. Let us not become conceited, competing against one another, envying one another. (Galatians 5:22–26)

The rules have changed, and the Galatians are born into freedom guided by the Spirit. While some are attempting to barter the righteousness of the Galatian believers in legalistic terms, Paul is advocating for a new way of being instead of the old way of doing. These are less measurable, perhaps, at least in objective terms, and yet, this fruit—the fruit of love— is also what Jesus points out as the signs of his followers (John 13:35). There in John 13, Peter is telling Jesus about all the things he will do, but Jesus gave him a different metric just before: love one another. It is not about what we can do for Jesus. It is about how we let the Spirit lead us in love.

Not about Peak Performance

Have you ever watched someone really thrive in their gifting? Have you seen them come alive and live fully into what they were created to do? It is beautiful to witness, but it can also be dangerous. Those of us in the white American evangelical church have seen this up close too many times. The talented and charismatic pastor draws big crowds, grows the church attendance numbers, and gets the book deals and speaking gigs. But though some of the gifts they utilize are born of or boosted by the Spirit, they can still fail to be a good and faithful disciple. Because there is "a still more excellent way" than being eager for greater gifts or even using yours in peak performance. Paul lays it out for us in 1 Corinthians 13:1–3:

If I speak in the tongues of humans and of angels but do not have love, I am a noisy gong or a clanging cymbal. And if I have prophetic powers and understand all mysteries and all knowledge and if I have all faith so as to remove mountains but do not have love, I am nothing. If I give away all my possessions and if I hand over my body so that I may boast but do not have love, I gain nothing.

We can appear to be at the top of our game, doing it all in the name of Jesus, and still be failing to follow him well. Because our faith is not a compartment of our lives. It encompasses our entire being, and love is the fuel that fires the engine of ourselves into true discipleship. We cannot leave our hearts behind. A love like Christ's must power any work we do for Christ, if we want to be true to our calling.

Believing, Behaving, Becoming

When we think of discipleship, oftentimes we think only of the knowledge side of the journey—how we are growing in our knowledge of God and the Scriptures. But this is only one piece of the discipleship puzzle. A disciple needs to be formed in what they believe (orthodoxy), what they do (orthopraxy), and what they become (orthopathy).[1]

Orthodoxy, or right beliefs, often focuses on instilling the proper doctrines and assumptions in our brothers and sisters. This is vital work, because theology should be a building block for the outworking of our faith. Orthopraxy, or right practices, includes everything from the rituals inside church worship services to the practical ways we live our faith through caring for others, evangelism, and even making disciples. Having proper beliefs should drive us to behave or practice our faith in ways that glorify God. And we tend to do a decent job of this, as well, even if sometimes our actions take a back seat to our beliefs. But many of us have left orthopathy, or right being, behind. I'm not sure we do it intentionally, but because we have emphasized other ways to measure a disciple's success, we have often confused orthopraxy with orthopathy. If we see right action or good results, we assume right belief and right being. But it's not always the case. We need all three to be fully formed disciples.

We put a lot of our focus on the first two pieces of the puzzle because they come straight out of those words of Jesus, in the great commission: "Go therefore and *make disciples* of all nations, baptizing them in the name of the Father and of the Son and of the Holy Spirit and *teaching them to obey everything that I have commanded you*" (Matthew 28:19–20a, emphasis added). This command shows both the head and the hands part of our work. But orthopathy, or right becoming or relating, goes beyond *what* we do and into *how* we do it. If we see the head and the hands aspects of discipleship in orthodoxy and orthopraxy respectively, it is in orthopathy that we see its heart. And as we saw in 1 Corinthians 13, even if everything else is technically correct, it can be rendered useless without proper love.

Love is the beginning of all the fruits of the Spirit. But these fruits are often cultivated through relationships and even conflict, and we haven't done well to fill up our toolkits with the necessary tools for constructive conflict with others. We need skills like emotional maturity, good communication, and healthy relationship practices.[2] Through these we learn to cultivate awareness of ourselves and those around us. In doing so, we can often see the Spirit remaking our inner being so we become better vessels of love to those around us.

Discipleship with these three elements is the process of remaking our character more like Christ, and as the old saying of Heraclitus goes, "Man's character is his fate."[3] Once our character is more closely conformed to Christ, the ways in which we behave and believe reflect him as well. Over time, we find ourselves equipped not only to believe and behave well but also to become—all of which are elements of becoming a fully formed disciple.

It Starts with Belonging

We all long to belong. It is one of those fundamental needs that we all seek out.[4] Discipleship that transforms lives and communities starts in a safe space to belong, and it is only through a safe community that we can begin this formation process. This belonging is so important because discipleship is the result of the work and influence of a chain of people—it takes many interactions with an idea in order to rework one's entire life to be more like Christ's.

The good news is that God designed the church—the community of God's people writ large—to live in this way. Since the beginning, discipleship and spiritual formation have not been solitary acts. We've unpacked some of that already when we talked about the metaphors Paul used to describe our connection and the meaning of our rituals. Discipleship of the whole person is only possible when we are the whole body of Christ working together.

What does this look like in practice? I think we can look once again to the church of Jerusalem in Acts 2:42–47 (CSB) and how they embodied the three "ortho-"s after Pentecost:

They devoted themselves to the apostles' teaching [orthodoxy], to the fellowship [orthopathy], to the breaking of bread, and to prayer [orthopraxy].

Everyone was filled with awe [orthopathy], and many wonders and signs were being performed through the apostles. Now all the believers were together and held all things in common. They sold their possessions and property and distributed the proceeds to all, as any had need [orthopraxy]. Every day they devoted themselves to meeting together in the temple, and broke bread from house to house [orthopraxy]. They ate their food with joyful and sincere hearts, praising God and enjoying the favor of all the people [orthopathy]. Every day the Lord added to their number those who were being saved.

We must care for every side of formation, because we need every side of formation. To leave one out is to leave behind part of our wholeness or integrity. As we seek wholeness together, we will often find ourselves becoming whole individually. But it only happens when we focus on every aspect of discipleship—shaping our head, hands, and hearts to be more like Christ's.

An example of this in my life is my husband's relationship with his mentor. Daniel and Butch met every Thursday morning for several years. They met at the church we were members of at the time and both participated in a Bible study group that eventually dissolved, but the two decided to keep meeting anyway. Butch didn't just know a lot, he lived well. He was quiet and kind—the kind of person who remembered your name, followed up on your prayer requests, and always wanted to know what you thought about something. He was the first to offer his home to those who needed a place to stay—whether it be for a night or for a year. I'm willing to bet that he gave assistance in ways he would never think to tell others about over the years.

Daniel learned a lot from Butch. He memorized Bible verses he didn't know before and unpacked what it means to be a disciple. Daniel learned more than Bible verses from Butch. He learned how to be friends with someone you don't agree with on everything, how to better open our home to meet others and their needs, and how to be on the lookout for ways to help those in front of us. And I learned by proxy. Butch loved Daniel, and we both love people better because we knew him. Butch was a fully formed disciple—even more so now that he's with Christ in eternity.

I have moved the goalposts for myself in a way that doesn't just focus on making me a better Christian, but in a way that also aims to make me a better human. For so much of my life, I felt like my humanness was at odds with my faith—that my flesh and my heart would always be fighting my mind, which was the place where faith was cultivated. Now I realize that my faith is part of what heals and restores the humanity in myself and helps me to uphold the dignity and humanity of others. I have better relationships, more empathy, and deeper compassion than I had before because I see that is all part of the work of becoming a disciple. The goal now is love, joy, peace, patience, kindness, goodness, faithfulness, gentleness, and self-control. And that will lead to a life well lived.

ELEVEN

In Spirit and in Truth

IT'S A WEIRD thing to be watched while you worship. But it's not exactly new for me. I used to work at summer cheerleading camps that had a Christian worship element, and the most comfortable way I've found through it is to close my eyes while everyone stares at me singing at the front while they sing the same song as close as ten feet away from me.

But this time I was half a world away, having that same experience. Except I wasn't singing in my language. It felt even stranger to be watched while I tried to follow the tune of the song and sing the English words I knew over the sounds of the language of the people in front of me. We were on a plain in East Africa, where several groups had gathered for worship. They had a common leader, but they didn't often worship together. And they certainly didn't worship with folks who look like me, because it's not often you see someone with my pale skin tone in their region. That was precisely why they wanted to honor us by giving us chairs at the front of their group instead of letting us take it all in from the back, as I would have preferred. But as uncomfortable as the experience was for me, I also have to admit, I was there to watch them worship too.

One of my favorite experiences everywhere I go is participating in worship in a different culture. It never ceases to amaze me how many expressions of worship there are around the world. I was raised very Southern Baptist, to the point that my Christian school didn't have a prom but a banquet because dancing wasn't allowed. Yet here, under the bright yellow sun, several of the groups prepared songs and dances to share to lead us all in worship together. It was lively and vibrant, and their enthusiasm for Jesus was palpable. You could not escape it. I loved the music and dancing, but my favorite part of worship that day came later.

Near the end of the service, there was a time of offering. This is pretty normal for many churches. In my church at the time, ushers would pass around offering plates where we each could lay our money during the designated window. Or we could wait and give online, or drop an envelope in one of the giving boxes at the back of our sanctuary.

But this community didn't have a sanctuary, or an offering plate for that matter. Instead, they moved one of the brightly colored plastic chairs, like the ones we had been sitting on, to the middle of the outdoor space we occupied. One by one, different people walked up and laid a variety of items on or around the chair. Food, animals, and gifts were all laid there as an offering for God and for the sake of the community. One woman walked up near the end, and quietly, as though she was trying not to be noticed, tenderly laid down small, handmade brooms on the chairs. These were what she had to give.

After the worship service, we spent the day interviewing people there to learn about their stories and their lives. At the end of each day, I would write some thoughts or insights in a note on my phone. That day, I wrote, "These people have nothing, and I think they love Jesus more because of it." It was so clear to me that their worship wasn't just about the singing and dancing. Their worship was wrapped up in who they were, to the point that they would give so much of what they had, which wasn't much, in worship of God and service of others. I wasn't sure what could eclipse the joyful and thoughtful worship they gave during the corporate worship service, but the worship that they gave in their everyday lives showed me what it meant to worship with their full selves.

The Idol of Worship

During the beginning of the COVID-19 pandemic here in the United States, we experienced some federal lockdown measures. This extended to our workplaces, leisure spaces, and houses of worship. The danger of gathering and breathing the same air as one another was now a danger to ourselves— in some cases, a lethal one. Many churches understood the gravity of this, but others saw it as infringing on their rights or ability to worship. So this small subset of churches decided to flout the restrictions we were all under and gather for worship anyway. They wanted to sing praise to God uninhibited by masks.[1] When the experts were saying the breath in our very lungs could be a danger to others, some then chose to weaponize their worship. I was left to wonder if worship that endangers its community and its neighbors could, indeed, be called worship at all.

In spaces like this, the form of worship became elevated over the function. Some churches chose buildings over people and making a spectacle of themselves over making much of God. As I watched these stories unfold on the news and on social media, I found myself angry and sad, because this seemed to push a particular kind of worship into the realm of idolatry. Idolatry often takes a good thing and makes it bigger or more important than it ought to be. In this case, the definition of worship had been so skewed by a cultural conception and a desire for a particular kind of freedom that it had ceased to become about God and instead became focused on the people themselves.

For much of my church experience, worship has meant a particular meeting time with a set agenda of activities. We sing, pray, listen to a sermon, give an offering, and maybe even participate in our shared rituals. This is worship. It has a time and a place. This is not without foundation; in the Hebrew Bible, singing, prayer, offering sacrifices, performing acts of piety like fasting, and listening to the Scriptures were all parts of worship.[2] But we also find in the Bible that worship is not limited to these corporate or personal activities, and that performing acts of worship with the wrong goal or spirit is to not worship at all.

The Bible spends a good deal of time addressing worship in a variety of ways—on a personal and a corporate level. God desires true worship, and true worship requires more than being in a certain place and performing the right activities. True worship, according to Scripture, is not location bound, and it is not compartmentalized to one part of our lives. We don't merely perform worship. We're also meant to live it.

Where We Worship

I have long loved the care and attention that Jesus gave to the woman at the well in Samaria. He could have, and most would have, skipped over this place and ignored this woman. Yet he sits with her, sees her, and gives her the keys to eternal life. During this conversation, she knows she is speaking to someone wise. She knows she has someone in front of her who can answer the questions that are burning on her heart. So she asks.

> The woman said to him, "Sir, I see that you are a prophet. Our ancestors worshiped on this mountain, but you say that the place where people must worship is in Jerusalem." Jesus said to her, "Woman, believe me, the hour is coming when you will worship the Father neither on this mountain nor in Jerusalem. You worship what you do not know; we worship what we know, for salvation is from the Jews. *But the hour is coming and is now here when the true worshipers will worship the Father in spirit and truth, for the Father seeks such as these to worship him.* (John 4:19–23, emphasis added)

At the time, Samaritans and Israelites were not on good terms. It's a surprise, really, that Jesus stops at the well at all. It is completely unexpected of him to do so. Part of the rift between the two ethnic groups was over where true worship happens. There are two mountains, and each group insists one is the valid place of worship and not the other, without relenting. The woman at the well wants to know where she can worship God. This is a vital question for her because she wants to worship God, and she wants to worship well. So at the top of her mind is a question of location, but Jesus changes the subject.

You see, God's priority is not where "official" worship takes place. Location isn't the site of true worship for God, especially not in this moment when Jesus has come and the Holy Spirit is coming soon. Jesus doesn't tell her which mountain because it doesn't matter as much now. What matters is that the worshiper worships "in spirit and in truth." True worship happens wherever that kind of worship happens.[3] It is not contained in a temple building or a particular mountain or even a specific people any longer.

This is good news for the Samaritan woman and for all of us. Though salvation came from the Jews through Christ, worship is not confined any longer. Her worship is counted faithful not because it's in the right place but because it's in the right state of being. To be "in spirit and in truth" is to be in wholeness, which is now possible in Christ. It is to seek the spiritual and physical good of ourselves and others. It is to be in alignment with the character and desires of God through Christ. Why we worship and how we live our worship matter as much as what we do in worship.

Why We Worship

"Every day, you're choosing which way you bow." I wrote that down on a church bulletin in college as my pastor said it. Though I was by all accounts a "good Christian girl," I knew that sometimes I was more concerned with being praised as the good Christian girl for my own sake than being good for God's sake. I knew sin was bad, and I wanted to avoid its painful consequences, of course, but I also just really liked being seen in the right light. Like the churches I spoke of before, my worship was sometimes about me. I still struggle at times, because my reputation is an easy idol to worship. But that kind of worship fails. It fails because it starts and ends with me, and, though I am a human being made in the image of God, I am not God and not worthy of worship.

In Romans, Paul paints this beautiful picture of the work and grace of God. He spends chapter after chapter unpacking what it means to be in Christ and how that changes our lives. In chapter 12, he takes a turn from the strictly theological and into the practical. You can tell because he drops a quick little "therefore" into his opening sentence: "I appeal to you therefore, brothers and sisters, on the basis of God's mercy, to present your bodies as a living sacrifice, holy and acceptable to God, which is your reasonable act of worship" (Romans 12:1).

Because of all God has done, and because the depth and riches of his wisdom are unknown and his mercy has been unleashed, we no longer need to offer sacrifices to appease our sin. Rather, we are to *be* the sacrifices as we live. Did you notice Paul describes this as "reasonable?" It seems like a big ask, right? But to Paul, who has spent so many words detailing the great mercy of God, to offer ourselves in full is a completely reasonable response to this mercy. It is not something to be done to earn righteousness. Nor is it to be done in order to be noticed. It is done as a reasonable act of worship. Because of God's mercy, God is worthy of our full-bodied worship, and worship begins when we recognize the goodness and greatness of our God. This is the basis of our worship. In fact, we sacrifice ourselves as an act of worship to God rather than build ourselves up in front of others.

Jesus' words in the Sermon on the Mount drive home the importance of the state of the heart in worship too. In Matthew 6, he discusses the personal acts of piety valued in Israelite society—giving to the poor, prayer, and fasting. But he begins the entire section with this warning: "Beware of practicing your righteousness before others in order to be seen by them, for then you have no reward from your Father in heaven" (Matthew 6:1).

And as he unpacks his examples, he gives us a new definition of hypocrisy as applied to these acts of worship. I tend to think of a hypocrite as one who says one thing but does another, but in the words of Jesus in Matthew 6, a hypocrite is one who does the good they are supposed to but for the wrong reasons.[4] The faithful and the hypocrite give to the poor, but the faithful give in secret and the hypocrite calls attention to themselves as they give. When it comes to prayer, the hypocrites stand up in public and babble on in order to be seen by others, but the faithful are to pray in secret in the simple example of Christ in the Lord's Prayer. The last example Jesus gives is fasting. The hypocrites walk around looking somber to have the opportunity to talk about their fasting. Again, those who are considered faithful instead try to look their best so their fasting is kept secret. Each by performing their worship has received their reward—some from people and some from God, some in public praise and some in secret, some today and some in the future hope of the kingdom.

Why we worship matters because it points to what we worship. If we seek to be glorified for our actions, we are actually seeking to be worshiped ourselves. But our reasonable act of worship is one of sacrifice, because the object of our worship is not ourselves but the only one worthy.

How We Live Worship

Right worship also encompasses the state of the lives in which our worship is situated. This doesn't mean that we need to have it all together to worship God. Spoiler alert: that isn't going to happen until restoration. Rather, it is important that we truly embody living sacrifices outside our houses of worship. True worship is also in how we live and love in our lives. The prophets in the Old Testament give us plenty of examples of what God wants from us in worship. The most famous is probably Micah 6:8, which says, "He has told you, O mortal, what is good, and what does the LORD require of you but to do justice and to love kindness and to walk humbly with your God?"

The rebukes of God delivered through the prophets tell us over and over that the failure of Israel is not one of performed piety but one of misplaced priorities everywhere else. In fact, performing piety without seeking the flourishing of all as commanded by God may render acts of worship unacceptable to God. Here's an example from Isaiah 58:1–5:

> Shout out; do not hold back!
>   Lift up your voice like a trumpet!
> Announce to my people their rebellion,
>   to the house of Jacob their sins.
> Yet day after day they seek me
>   and delight to know my ways,
> as if they were a nation that practiced righteousness
>   and did not forsake the ordinance of their God;
> they ask of me righteous judgments;
>   they want God on their side.
> "Why do we fast, but you do not see?
>   Why humble ourselves, but you do not notice?"

> Look, you serve your own interest on your fast day
>> and oppress all your workers.
> You fast only to quarrel and to fight
>> and to strike with a wicked fist.
> Such fasting as you do today
>> will not make your voice heard on high.
> Is such the fast that I choose,
>> a day to humble oneself?
> Is it to bow down the head like a bulrush
>> and to lie in sackcloth and ashes?
> Will you call this a fast,
>> a day acceptable to the LORD?

This is a stern rebuke! God is telling the prophet to let loose, to tell the people exactly why they fall short. On paper, it seemed like they performed all the right tasks and followed all the major rules. Yet it didn't seem like God was listening to them. Their fasting and praying was ineffective, and they wanted to know why. Yes, fasting, prayer, and other worship are what God asked of them, but it was not *all* God asked of them. They did not fulfill the whole brief of worship. They were not a people who "practiced righteousness." Instead they served their own interests, oppressed those working for them, and quarreled. This was not the kind of fasting God asked of them. It was not the kind of worship that brings God glory or seeks the good of another. It was unrecognizable to God.

But God doesn't leave them without options. The writer of this part of Isaiah recounts the message of what kind of fast God's looking for in the second half of Isaiah 58. The worship God desires looks like:

- Loosing the bonds of injustice

- Letting the oppressed go free

- Sharing bread with hungry

- Bringing the poor into your house

- Covering the naked

- Not hiding from your own kin

That kind of worship will result in God hearing their call and answering them with healing and victory. It is that kind of worship in which God can say, "I am here." All other worship that fails to seek justice in the world around them serves to hinder true worship. Any acts of worship or piety of God's people that are not done in alignment with the desires of God in the rest of their lives are not worshipful at all. God wants obedience in our lives. If our bodies are living sacrifices, then what we do in our bodies, and especially how we love our neighbors, become key ways that we love and worship God.

Carrying the Lord's Name

I went to Bible college for my junior year of my undergraduate studies. Before I came to that campus, I was the go-to Christian gal in my circles. But there I felt out of my league. More than once that year, I stood in a chapel surrounded by other believers raising their hands in worship and singing that year's Chris Tomlin hit at the top of their lungs while tears began to form in their eyes and roll down their cheeks. I didn't usually—if ever—experience God that way. I experienced God's love with my mind, not my emotions. I devoured

Christian nonfiction for fun. I bought commentaries and concordances, and my favorite assignments were our exegetical papers in my undergrad theology classes.

But over and over as I watched my peers worship with their emotions on display, doubts began to creep in . . . was my worship as good as theirs? Was I missing something because I didn't "feel" God in the same way others did? I did cry tears, but they were tears desperate to be like everyone else . . . tears that fell down my face as I prayed that God would make my worship as good as theirs. I didn't realize that would be the start of a journey to understanding that worship isn't all emotions and raised hands while singing. It's so much more about how I carried God with me in my life inside and outside the chapel walls.

There has been a lot of discourse over the last few years about what it means to take the Lord's name in vain. As children, a lot of us good evangelical kids were taught that it meant to use God's name frivolously in our speech. Now, I don't think that's wrong, but I have come to believe it's not totally right, either. The word for *vain* used in this prohibition in the Ten Commandments refers to unreality or emptiness, and the word for *take* is actually the word *lift* or *carry*.[5] You might even say *take* means "to bear," as in "bearing God's image." To not take the Lord's name in vain is more than what we say. It is also to not misuse God's name in our insincere or frivolous deeds. Every person bears God's image, and as those in Christ who are part of God's family we also bear God's name. What we do, how we do it, and why we do it are all places where we have the potential to misuse God's name by putting it on something God does not desire nor would approve.

This feels especially applicable in the discussion of how we seek to worship God, because when we worship we put God's name on our lips, our hearts, and our actions. We need to be sure that as we carry the Lord's name with us, we do so in a worthy manner. Our worship can't be shallow or for our own praise. It can't be compartmentalized to a few hours a week, and it can't be tied to one location or set of practices. We always carry the name of God with us, and therefore, we are always worshiping. The question we must be vigilant about asking is: Are we worshiping in spirit and in truth?

Though it is undoubtedly a higher standard for worship than the emotional connection I sought back in college, this idea set me free. I could not only engage in worship wherever I happened to be, but I could also worship in the way that I am best suited. My worship was good enough even without tears and raised hands. Whenever, wherever, and however I carry the name of the Lord well, I am worshiping and so are you.

TWELVE

The Ties That Bind Us

ONE DAY IN East Africa we drove to the river, because today was the day that several churches in the area were gathering to baptize new believers. These new believers had been waiting awhile to be baptized. The closest body of water where they could fully immerse adults wasn't exactly close. They were willing to wait to not only make the trek to be baptized but also to have the other people in communities nearby come to celebrate with them. Although we weren't from a nearby community, the others on the trip and I were able to celebrate with them too.

We drove for hours in the middle of a hot day full of listening to and in turn encouraging local churches, but this baptism service was a bright spot for me. There, in a river dyed red by the dirt underneath it, I peeked over the green plants as I sat on a patch of grass to watch a new believer be baptized.

"In the name of the Father, the Son, and the Holy Spirit. Buried with Christ and raised to walk in newness of life."

The people who came to witness this blessed event clapped and cheered. It was a ritual they too had once experienced. It was part of the language of their faith, our faith. That's what rituals are. They are intentional practices that signify, enact, or communicate something within a group. Rituals aren't necessarily hollow or silly or evil. They are a way we connect to one another and pass on our faith.

When I worked for myself for a time, I tried to follow a lot of gurus who could help me be as successful as possible. Creating a morning routine was a popular piece of advice I encountered. Entire books have been written on it, like *The Miracle Morning* or *The 5 AM Club*. They promised this ritual or routine would be my secret to being the best version of myself during the day. It would unlock all my potential and help me conquer my tasks and have a more spacious life. This routine wouldn't be for anyone else. It would be for me. It was mine to own, to enact, and to succeed in.

I remember as a young person how the language used to describe the rituals of our faith—and I use *rituals* not out of disrespect but for simplicity as different traditions use different terms—felt a bit like the morning routine talk of my entrepreneurial days. Baptism was "a celebration of my personal decision." It was my Christian welcome party, a public profession of an inward reality. My private decision to follow Jesus was now public, and everyone who gathered celebrated me and my personal faith. Similar language was used before communion. It was about "coming clean about my sins" and "making myself right with God." I needed to be sure I believed and that I had confessed all the sins I could think of and even what I couldn't, because if I didn't mean it, I would be worse off than before. The rituals were done publicly, but they were meant for me personally.

For many of the believers I met overseas, a big public baptism didn't work. Whether they lacked a big enough body of water, more than another believer or two in their community, or the safety to make a major confession of faith in areas with no church buildings and little privacy, they had to seek different ways of participating. Sometimes this looked like their friend baptizing them in their own bathtub or next to the well. I found the same thing with communion. Grape juice and fancy bread or crackers aren't available everywhere. In those places, elements took the form of water, tea, local bread, or processed peanut butter crackers. People found ways to be creative. Their witness has shown me that the ritual is the key, not necessarily the elements themselves (though I know some will disagree with that last bit, and that's okay).[1]

And if that's the case, what does it mean to be faithful to the ritual even when you have to get a little creative about the means? Of the many questions I had when it came to these two sacred rituals of our faith, at the top of the list was, "What are they for *anyway*?" It turns out that like most things in Christianity, as much as there's a "me" element to it, there is also a "we" element.

An Invitation to Intimacy

We love to debate our shared Christian rituals. There are a whole lot of how and what questions that various traditions answer differently, but we won't be tackling those as much here. I think the more important question is *why*. It is easy to then take that on with a simple, "Because Jesus said so," and indeed, he did. *Repent, believe, and be baptized* were some of his more clear and simple commands. It helps that we see him being baptized as well. If we're following in the steps and words of Jesus, as I often advocate, then baptism ought to be in the mix. But if the apostle Paul is to be believed as well, and I think he is, there is more to the story than asking "What would Jesus do?" One thing baptism does that we all tend to agree on is that it's actually a way we enter into unity with Christ and with one another. Paul's letter to the Romans tells this to us.

Unity with Christ

Do you not know that all of us who were baptized into Christ Jesus were baptized into his death? Therefore we were buried with him by baptism into death, so that, just as Christ was raised from the dead by the glory of the Father, so we also might walk in newness of life.

For if we have been united with him in a death like his, we will certainly be united with him in a resurrection like his. (Romans 6:3–5)

Baptism is both visible and invisible. In the visible realm, we see the person being baptized, the person performing the baptism, and the water of baptism, along with whatever family and friends are there to witness. But whether at the moment of the baptism itself or at the time of belief before ever entering the water, there are invisible elements at work, too—a spiritual cleansing and a Spirit embodying. We as regular Joes and Janes find ourselves connected to the divine when we are connected to the waters of baptism. Paul echoes this idea in 1 Corinthians 12:13, saying, "For in the one Spirit we were *all baptized into one body*—Jews or Greeks, slaves or free—and we were all made to drink of one Spirit" (emphasis added). St. Augustine saw this as more than a metaphor, as a true union, especially in light of how he interprets Acts 9:34 when Christ stops Paul on the road to Damascus:

> The head about to ascend into heaven commended to us His members on earth and departed. Thenceforth, you find not Christ speaking on earth; you find Him speaking, but from heaven. And even from heaven, why? Because his members on earth were trodden upon. For to the persecutor Saul, he said from on high, 'Saul, Saul, why do you persecute me?' . . . 'For I ascend, because I am the Head: my Body lies yet beneath. Where lies? Throughout the whole earth. Beware you strike not, beware you hurt not, beware you trample not.' These are the last words of Christ about to go into heaven."[2]

This union was a true, spiritual reality to Augustine. Christ is the head, and the church is his body. And though Christ is the Lord and authority, this really emphasizes unity, not hierarchy. The head is above in the heavenly realm, and his body lives his purposes on earth and, indeed, the suffering and experiences of that body are felt in the head. This was called the *totus Christus*,[3] the full body of Christ, which mirrors the divinity fused with humanity in the incarnation of Christ. We are not separate from Christ. We are in Christ. We are part of him. Whatever you believe about how and when that happens through baptism, we all see it as the way we are grafted in as a member of Christ's body, which firmly places us within the family of God.

Unity with Each Other

For as in one body we have many members and not all the members have the same function, *so we, who are many, are one body in Christ, and individually we are members one of another.* We have gifts that differ according to the grace given to us: prophecy, in proportion to faith; ministry, in ministering; the teacher, in teaching; the encourager, in encouragement; the giver, in sincerity; the leader, in diligence; the compassionate, in cheerfulness. (Romans 12:4–8, emphasis added)

Paul loves to use this image of the body. It crops up here, and again in Corinthians and in Ephesians. It paints such an interesting picture of the ways in which we are connected and dependent upon one another as a community. We are not just invited into Christ, but we are also invited into an interconnected system, a community committed to mutual flourishing for each other and our neighbors. This kind of community is often the miracle we need to meet the needs around us. Not one of us can be on our own and flourish. It takes a village—well, a whole body.

This is why we cannot live the life of faith alone. We each have our own gifts and resources, but they aren't enough— they weren't intended to be. We are one part of an ecosystem that depends on every other part of the ecosystem to create an environment for flourishing. It is our invitation to a new kind of intimacy. God called a *people* for Godself, not a single person. Even the people who were called out individually, like Adam and Eve or Moses or Abraham, were called for the sake of God's people—so that current and future generations might follow God in a flourishing community based on God's economy. It is through our unity with Christ that we find ourselves able to support one another as we walk in God's way. We are bound by our one baptism. And through those waters, we are invited to be as close to each other as our eyes are to our ears, our hands to our feet, our hearts to our minds. We rely on one another to be our fullest selves and live out our calling as the people of God. The family of God begins at baptism.

An Invitation to Integrity

We begin together at baptism. The very beginning sparks of intimacy are born at that time that we and the church body commit to one another through those sacred waters. But when we talk about this kind of intimacy, we can get uncomfortable for a few reasons.

First, this idea of dependence has sometimes been taken to extremes and enforced in unhealthy ways, especially in spiritually abusive places. Toxicity and sin corrupt what God designed, as they always do. It takes God's good and twists and perverts it, and when this happens, those who have been abused might need to seek safety outside the bounds of community for a time.

Second, this idea of intimacy and reliance also fights against the values of a rugged American individualism. How often do we sing the praises of those who pulled themselves up by their bootstraps? We love a story of someone who worked hard and made it through, perhaps even made it to the top. But God's design for humanity is communal, not individual. Even in the beginning, God made Adam and Eve to mutually support each other and work with one another. It is not good for a human to be alone, they remind us. Our baptism beckons us into the intimacy of community.

Failing to Keep Our Commitments

In the same way, communion is an invitation to examine and maintain the integrity of that community:

> Whoever, therefore, eats the bread or drinks the cup of the Lord in an unworthy manner will be answerable for the body and blood of the Lord. Examine yourselves, and only then eat of the bread and drink of the cup. For all who eat and drink without discerning the body eat and drink judgment against themselves. (1 Corinthians 11:27–29)

In the preceding verses of this familiar passage, Paul is very directly unpacking what he views as an abuse of communion. At the time, this kind of ritual often took place as part of a meal together. It was meant to be a picture of the community of God and point toward our shared future, but the Corinthians had taken to separating themselves on what appear to be social and economic lines. Some would have a great meal with wine while others were left in need. Communion was meant as a reminder of the death of Christ and what that means for everyone at the table, of their bond formed at baptism and enacted every day. But some of the groups had broken those bonds. They were observing the ritual, but they stripped it of its meaning when they failed to uphold their community commitments, as biblical scholar Gordon Fee points out:

The Corinthian problem was not their failure to gather, but their failure truly to be God's newly formed people when they assembled; here there was to be neither Jew nor Greek, slave nor free (cf. 12:13), and as the present context strongly suggests, neither rich nor poor.[4]

Communion is more than just our opportunity to make ourselves right with God, though I certainly think that is part of it. It's about making ourselves right with each other. In the Sermon on the Mount, Jesus talks about bringing a gift to the altar only after reconciling with someone with whom you have issues. This has parallels to the Corinthians approaching their participation in the remembrance of Christ's sacrifice in an unworthy way. When they approach the table without having made other relationships right as well, they are poorly embodying the body of Christ—the same body that they are celebrating being broken for them. They are not working to heal and reconcile the body. They are allowing the world's categories to separate their community instead of following the movement of the equalizing forces of God's family.

Most often, we think of integrity as our character—"strong moral principles"—but the Oxford dictionary offers a second definition, and it's my favorite: "the state of being whole and undivided." Communion is the place we bring ourselves to not just remember Christ but also to re-member his body.[5] This is the table where we feast together and are made whole, where we regain our integrity. This is the table at which we are healed, but that is in vain if we do not repent of the ways in which we have wounded one another. This is the place we reconcile, through the blood of Christ, and we recommit to uphold our integrity in the intimacy of community. This is the place where we meet each other and the Spirit to make right what is wrong, and we must begin with restoring our communal integrity. Communion provides the perfect back-drop for this reconciling work.

Finding Our Way Back to Wholeness

He himself is before all things, and in him all things hold together. He is the head of the body, the church; he is the beginning, the firstborn from the dead, so that he might come to have first place in everything. For in him all the fullness of God was pleased to dwell, and through him *God was pleased to reconcile to himself all things, whether on earth or in heaven, by making peace through the blood of his cross.*

And you who were once estranged and hostile in mind, doing evil deeds, he has now reconciled in his fleshly body through death, so as to present you holy and blameless and irreproachable before him . . . (Colossians 1:17–22, emphasis added)

In this passage, Paul paints a pretty gruesome picture of what it takes to reconcile. The way for reconciliation has been made through the blood of the cross. The blood we drink and the body we eat—whether you believe that is physically or symbolically or something in between—has reconciled us to God. In the same way, it is a vehicle for reconciliation with each other. When we examine the body as we approach the table, we must remember that includes not just our personal lives and sins, but also the sin we commit toward and as the community.

Communion carves out an opportunity to ensure we are bringing our whole selves to the table. It is a chance to take a beat and ask ourselves where we are failing each other. Are we feasting in one section and leaving others starved in another? Are we taking what is holy and using it as an opportunity to profane ourselves by oppressing others? Where do we need to confess, repair, and reconcile with one another? By seeking reconciliation, we are honoring the sacrifice that first reconciled us. This is where our wholeness, our integrity, can be reborn. Through the bread and the wine, we are beckoned back to the waters of our baptism and the covenant we make as a community.

We don't just need these rituals for our personal faith, and they're not actually designed to be for that, either. The way we most fully embody the rituals is to remember what they mean for us as a community. They are not a mere performance in the art of holiness or tools for our personal righteousness. They are tools for our participation in the story and family of God. They are the practice we require to fulfill the life of intimacy and integrity in community we are called to.

My husband and I have a ritual to celebrate something exciting in our lives—new jobs, graduations, book deals and more. We have champagne and tacos for dinner. It started back when my husband got a new job that would significantly help us in our first year of marriage. We went to Mi Cocina for a taco dinner, and we bought a bottle of champagne that wasn't on the lowest shelf of the grocery store. That day, a tradition was born. Now whenever something good happens, we need only to put the champagne and taco emojis into a text message to share the news. It's not big or flashy. I don't even think we've spent as much on this ritual as we did that first day. But even when it's not convenient or not a huge change, we still make time to celebrate. It's a ritual of remembrance. This ritual reminds us to practice gratitude for where we are and from where we've come. It holds us steady in a big time of change, and it gives us hope for what's to come.

It seems silly perhaps, but in a lot of ways, it's similar to how I think of our shared rituals in the church. They give us a place to belong and a way to mark our commitment to each other. It's not about personal guilt or condemnation. It's not about making sure that I've got my bases covered before the Lord. It's about our common hope and work. It's about reconciling with each other in here so we can be ministers of reconciliation out there. These rituals give us the moments of reflection we need to practice what we preach. They hold us together, and they mark out our mission to embody Christ in the world. And in that way, I've found they hold me to Christ who holds me together too.

THIRTEEN

Valuing Connection over Conversion

VIBRANT COLORS, DELICIOUS food, and warm smiles—these aren't things I associated with the Middle East until I went there. It wasn't just these things that made me love it, though the city I visited is now my favorite city in the world for its culture and variety. It was also the people with whom I got to experience the city. It sounds trite to say that my favorite thing about a place is the people, but it's pretty much always true. The people make the place.

In this case, the people I stayed with were a group of missionaries living there long-term to plant local churches. They had been there a couple of years by the time I visited, and by any normal metrics their work did not look successful. They had not really planted any churches yet, there were not a whole lot of people who now followed Jesus, they could not point to a lot of big and tangible ministry results. But they did have two things that impressed me immensely. They had a handful of really deep relationships within their community, and they had extraordinary closeness as a community of expatriates living and ministering together. It wasn't something just I noticed, but something others were noticing too. In a culture where hospitality is a norm but family is still deeply tied to biological bonds, and where ethnic acceptance is largely tied to a religious identity, this group of unrelated people was operating as a family, and that was special.

In this place, where religious identity was tied so closely to national and ethnic identities, it was also hard to go against the religious tide. What we think of traditionally as evangelism wasn't an option. Preaching on street corners? Nope. Handing out tracts? Uh-uh. Holding big, revival-style meetings to draw people in? No way. The work here was different. It was like good barbecue—made low and slow. These Christians had jobs here within their fields of expertise. They hung out at local places, and they made friends with their neighbors. They hoped to have opportunities to share Jesus, but these were not transactional relationships. They were real ones, and it illustrated to me what it might mean to live my witness in a way that I hadn't really experienced before. That not everything has to be for the sake of conversion. That every relationship matters, even if I don't see every person I meet start to follow Jesus too. And that while the mission matters, it is not meant to alienate but to invite into a loving community whether or not they would believe.

Heavy Burdens

I used to live in a world of "gospel-driven" everything. Don't get me wrong, I am obsessed with the gospel—I believe now more than ever that it is actually good news. But with that relentless focus came a lot of heavy burdens that put me in a pressure-filled spiral, afraid that I was never doing enough to evangelize, to share the gospel with anyone and everyone around me. Did I ask my restaurant server how I could pray for them when they brought my food out? Should I have chatted more with the grocery store clerk so I could tell them about Jesus? Did I walk my dog at the optimal time to see people in my neighborhood to talk to them about the gospel? I analyzed every interaction and opportunity, and no matter how much I wanted to be doing enough I never measured up to what I believed the standard to be.

Before I knew it, I found my confidence overtaken with social anxiety—I felt stressed about every potential conversation, depressed every time I didn't bring up the gospel because it didn't feel right in the moment, and wondered if I even loved people like I said I did if I couldn't even do this one thing for them. In those moments, the gospel didn't feel like very good news for me. As I began to realize the gospel sets us free rather than binds us to more rules, I set to work to rewire my own thoughts about evangelism. But first I had to remove a few of the burdens I had been carrying around on my gospel-driven shoulders.

The first burden I had to remove was the idea that I had to find or force a conversion moment. In that world, I found that I was always walking around hoping to be the last stop on someone's salvation journey. I wanted to get credit for that last moment before they said yes. Because if I wasn't winning souls, then what good was I to the kingdom anyway? I had to find the moments where people were ready and push to get them in the right place, and I could argue them down with all my apologetics skills if I needed to.

Being there to guide them through the moment of conversion was the important part, but even that was hard because I myself don't remember a specific moment of conversion. At some point it was pretty clear that I was really into Jesus, and as that grew, I oriented my life around him. But in my evangelical school growing up, I was surrounded by people who could tell you what they were wearing and where they were standing when they heard the gospel and responded. I felt insecure because I couldn't remember that, so for the sake of others' security, it was important to give them the moment.

But discipleship doesn't always work that way, and often it begins before someone is all in with a yes. It's why we teach kids at our churches! We believe that guiding them in the way of Jesus matters even if they don't yet (or maybe won't ever) believe. The same is true for adult relationships. We can help people live a kingdom kind of life even before they believe by living a kingdom life ourselves, and it might just be that the fruit of that—in our life and theirs—is their own belief.

The second burden I bore was the idea that I was responsible for sharing the gospel with every person I ever met because I may be "the only Jesus they ever meet." If you're (a) anxious and (b) a high performer like me, this is a recipe for disaster. Because now someone's eternity is always in your hands. The pressure is on at every moment to not just perform your faith well but also to proclaim your faith loudly everywhere you go and to every person you meet. I absolutely buckled under that pressure.

What I realized was that I was taking on the Holy Spirit's work. I do not change someone's heart. The Spirit does. My job is to live my witness and share when I feel prompted by the Spirit, but most often for me that has happened only in the context of long-term relationships when I wasn't really expecting it. I am one person or interaction in a long list of interactions, people, experiences, and nudges the Spirit may be working on. I may plant, someone else may water, but God gives the growth, as Paul reminds us (1 Corinthians 3:6).

The final burden I had to remove is the idea that I was responsible for making everyone believe exactly as I did. There is a strange kind of isolationism in the branch of evangelicalism in which I was formed. I didn't know much about other Christian traditions, but I knew that if whatever they said or did differed from my perspective then they were obviously wrong. I feared for my Catholic friends' salvation. I argued with my Methodist friends about the right way and time to baptize. And I eschewed every other viewpoint that didn't perfectly line up with mine. It is interesting that in a tradition that doesn't hold people to a creed or confession of faith, many shibboleths determined who was in and who was out.

I've become much more ecumenical in my approach for a few reasons. First, the evangelical tradition is relatively new compared to others. Second, Christian traditions actually have a lot in common if we hold to the basic articles of the faith—the orthodoxy we talked about in an earlier chapter. When we recognize the human-made parts of our traditions and that also we can't all be right, it becomes a lot easier to hold it all humbly. If we're on the same page about Jesus, then I'm good with that. I don't need to convert anyone to my particular way of thinking. There is space for all of us inside the big tent of Christianity, and removing those burdens helped free me to evangelize with joy and without time restraints—at home and anywhere in the world I may find myself.

Rooted in Relationships

When I want to find a good place to eat or which store has a particular item, I do something simple: I ask my friends. And you know what else? If I love something, I will often just tell my friends about it—the new app I use, the game I play, the makeup I found, the person I follow on social media. We are evangelists about things we love all the time. So why does it get weird when it comes to Jesus?

I may be in the minority here among those who are shaking up their beliefs and practices as they walk out of or seek to reform American evangelicalism, but I don't think evangelism is bad in itself. I find it really challenging to look at the life of Jesus and the witness of the early saints and say that proclaiming the good news is *not* something Christians are to participate in. Often it has been done poorly and even harmfully over the years (I include my own efforts here), and I lament that. The focus has become about souls over bodies, rather than the reintegration of the two. Evangelism has been boiled down to saying the right words so that you can know that you have done your part. But good, healthy evangelism is more than a message.

According to practical theologian Priscilla Pope-Levison, there are five key qualities of good evangelism: hospitality, relationship, integrity, message bearing, and church rootedness.[1] When we look at our own lives, we may see that these qualities made the most difference for us as well. And though they can be applied to mass evangelism events, note that most of those keys are not momentary—they require a life saturated with the gospel, the whole gospel. They require us to have deep ties to Jesus, a community of believers, and our neighbors.

We love to hold up Paul as a traveling preacher who stood in marketplaces and on banks of rivers to tell others about Jesus, but there are parts of Acts where we see him staying in a place for a long time to share the message:

> He entered the synagogue and for three months spoke out boldly and argued persuasively about the kingdom of God. When some stubbornly refused to believe and spoke evil of the Way before the congregation, he left them, taking the disciples with him, and argued daily in the lecture hall of Tyrannus. This continued for two years, so that all the residents of Asia, both Jews and Greeks, heard the word of the Lord. (Acts 19:8–10)

Sure, Paul spoke persuasively, but he also put down roots in a community. He stayed and cultivated relationships there. He was bold in sharing his message, but he didn't seek to be in and out of people's lives. When he could be there for a while without being killed or plotted against, he did, because deep connection matters. We see this same kind of dynamic in the way Christ sent out people as well:

> He said to them, "The harvest is plentiful, but the laborers are few; therefore ask the Lord of the harvest to send out laborers into his harvest. Go on your way; I am sending you out like lambs into the midst of wolves. Carry no purse, no bag, no sandals, and greet no one on the road. Whatever house you enter, first say, 'Peace to this house!' And if a person of peace is there, your peace will rest on that person, but if not, it will return to you. Remain in the same house, eating and drinking whatever they provide,

for the laborer deserves to be paid. Do not move about from house to house. Whenever you enter a town and its people welcome you, eat what is set before you; cure the sick who are there, and say to them, 'The kingdom of God has come near to you.'" (Luke 10:2–9)

Jesus' model of evangelism was to stay, develop relationships, and bring the holistic witness of the kingdom of God in that place. This is not short-term, in-and-out work. It is long, deep, and abiding. It is relational and holistic, and I think especially in today's context—where trust in Christians is low—that is what is required.

Our world is different from the ancient Near Eastern culture of Jesus or Paul. If you live in the United States like I do, you live in a place that is saturated with churches and messages about Jesus proclaimed by those who identify themselves as Christians. For better or worse, Christianity already has a reputation. A lot of people have heard about Jesus, and a lot of people don't care, because sometimes Christians can be terrible.

While we can draw a lot from the examples of Jesus and Paul, this moment has different challenges and thus requires different tools and approaches. Evangelism often means disentangling ourselves and helping others to disentangle Jesus from some false perceptions. We do this not coercively, but by living well, by being a part of the local community, making friends, and loving all people, knowing that you are one interaction along a journey that the Holy Spirit may be orchestrating in a life.[2] The pressure is not on you to be the only one to share. Sometimes your role is just to love. As evangelism expert Rick Richardson writes, "We belong to bless."[3] The job of evangelism is often just inviting people into relationships with us as human beings who care about and long to connect with other human beings.

To be an evangelist is to be a friend, to live your life as though your faith matters, and to be ready if people have questions or want to have conversations about that. Evangelism is not about transactions like giving someone food but requiring them to sit through a sermon first, or leaving people behind if they decide not to follow Jesus, or forcing them into making those choices because you're trying to meet a goal you've set for yourself. We can live out the gospel by being a good friend—always with hope but never with agenda.

Contextualization over Assimilation

We tend to refer to evangelistic efforts outside of our own communities as missions work, and this comes with its own set of cultural baggage. Many early Western missions efforts were closely tied with colonization efforts that sought to "civilize," Christianize, and control lands for empire.[4] As Anglican bishop and missionary scholar Stephen Neill wrote in his book *Colonialism and Christian Missions*, "The ideas of conquest and of conversion lay side by side in the consciousness of the Christians of the Western world."[5]

Though Christianity reached Africa and South Asia before it reached the West,[6] the British presence in several nations in North America and Africa and the Spanish and Portuguese efforts in South America were driven by a desire to grow their empires that often was camouflaged by a desire to evangelize. Many times this resulted in awful violence against the indigenous populations. One very disturbing account of this can be found in a book called *A Brief Account of the Destruction of the Indies*, by Bartolomé de las Casas. In it, he describes the awful ways the mission of God was used by one culture as an excuse to conquer and force assimilation of a foreign culture for wealth, power, and influence.[7]

This even extended into our more modern missions movements. Those outside of the Western world were considered "heathens" to be evangelized.[8] This evangelization was often in service of the larger goal of making them conform to European or American ideals, driven by the idea of the dominating culture's supremacy—which was largely tied to white racial ideals.[9]

Though it is subtle and often unconscious, white supremacy is still a part of many missions efforts. In some evangelical traditions, women are not allowed to teach or train men in congregations in the United States, but women can go overseas to do missions work that may include teaching and training, which carries an underlying idea that other nations or ethnicities may be "less than." Efforts not focused primarily on evangelism but on service can also demonstrate implicit white supremacy, like Christian missionaries who establish healthcare facilities in foreign nations without qualifications and do irreparable harm to people.[10]

White supremacy doesn't just affect those ministered to on the other side of the world. The support-raised missionary model that many missions organizations employ doesn't work as well for ethnic minorities in the United States.[11] A majority of missions organizations lack ethnic and cultural diversity, which can lead to one type of American experience being the standard. While not directly seeking to subjugate other nations or people, these are examples of the ways that missions work today can still be doing the work of white supremacy and Western assimilation.

There is another way. When we look at the goal of missions work as not assimilation but contextualization, we remove ourselves and our cultural preferences from the driver's seat. We can be the fuel, but we are not the ones driving. This requires a commitment to listening to and empowering the local people we serve.

In fact, it looks a lot like the Acts 6 community at work. In this chapter, the community of believers in Jerusalem was doing the work of caring for the orphans and widows. There was a problem, though, because the leaders were mostly Hebraic (Israel) Jews who were leaving the Hellenistic (Greek world) Jews out of their ministry. When someone noticed, the leaders got together and realized they needed more help to actually meet those needs. So they appointed others to be over this ministry to Hellenistic Jews, and all the names listed are Hellenistic names.[12] They trusted to the Hellenistic Jews the ministry for the Hellenistic Jews. Those who know the best way to meet the needs of a people are from that people.

Just like evangelism does at home, this requires relationships and long-term commitment, and even more, it requires partnership and being willing to not be at the front. This allows the ministry of the gospel—both the care of the community and the aspects of faith and worship—to take form in a culturally appropriate way.

So when it comes to missions work anywhere, but especially overseas, we need to ask ourselves some specific questions like . . .

- Is this work meeting physical needs and spiritual needs?

- Is this a long-term commitment?

- Are the people or organization qualified to do this work?

- Are we committed to listening to and empowering locals to lead?

- Are we willing to do the messy and small work as directed by qualified local people?

- Is our help actually needed, or are we projecting our supremacy by ignoring a base presence of Christianity that is taking a different expression than ours?

This isn't a comprehensive list, but it can help us begin developing the postures that allow us to have the conversation we need to be having.

Several years ago, my husband and I went to one of our favorite beer taprooms and saw they were going to offer a trivia night there once a week. We invited some acquaintances to join us, and our trivia team was born. It's been about eight years now, which I can hardly believe, but that weekly rhythm has become a weekly Bible study. It functionally served as our church during the worst of the COVID-19 pandemic when we moved it into our homes for a weekly game night, and even opened a safe space for a few of our non-Christian trivia friends to ask questions about God or the Bible if they want to. It was accidental, but the more we just became friends, understood the culture, and extended invitations to curious and friendly people, we found that we had opportunities to be the gospel in a bar every week.

I still think it's good to be gospel-driven, as long as we know that the gospel is more than the saying the right words and that we as individuals don't bear the sole responsibility

for its success. Jesus wants us to share in his work of proclamation and justice. These are not separate but one mission. It
involves caring for needs, developing friendships, and being
rooted and attentive where we are. Only with those tools do
we have the ability to bear witness to the whole gospel.

We don't have to focus on our past failures or on the future
fates of our friends to share the gospel. We can be present,
attentive, and joyful, because the consistency of our care
and character matters as much as our verbal witness. We are
whole people working toward a whole world, and we cannot
leave parts of others behind in our evangelism. We must be
committed to being a holistic witness for Jesus in the world—
at home and abroad. In the same way, this frees us to be our
whole selves. And as we do that, we will likely find that we
aren't just sharing the good news, we're living it.

Conclusion

ONE OF MY favorite cities in all the world is Istanbul. There is something fascinating about a city that holds many things together in one place. The large spice bazaar in the heart of the city gives you all the Middle Eastern vibes you could want—full of tapestries, tea rooms, and Turkish delight. Then you find yourself in another part of the city, and walking by the river feels like you're in France. European architecture and outdoor cafés, stone instead of tile, pastels instead of jewel tones. It feels like two different worlds in one city .

The Hagia Sophia is perhaps one of the best examples of these worlds converging. Built as an Eastern Orthodox church, it had the icons, mosaics, and architecture that were designed to tell the story of God for those who came to worship there. It was even the center of Orthodox Christianity until 1453, when the city fell to the Ottoman Empire and the building was converted into a mosque. Christian mosaics were covered, murals painted over, and Islamic calligraphy placed prominently. In 1935, it ceased to be a place of worship altogether. It's a museum, a relic of religion past and present. As restorations continue, new murals and mosaics are uncovered and restored, existing alongside the remaining signs of the Muslim faith. Since I am not able to visit very often, there is fresh potential with every visit that something old will be excavated and restored.

Some days my faith feels a bit like the Hagia Sophia. The building is the same, but the insides have changed over time. Past and present sometimes coexist or even overlap, but there's still a lot to uncover and restore. It's taken time to get here, and it'll take time to get to the next place—to find more beauty under the plaster and paint. Though the differences between my past and present are not as stark as between Islam and Christianity, the remnants of both versions of my faith remain. The temptation may be to turn my faith into a museum—a place to admire and appreciate but because of its history leave worship in the past. Instead, like a cathedral elsewhere, I've decided to let the beauty of both be a reminder to worship today, knowing that my relationship to God was carefully crafted and restored along the way.

We started the work in these pages. We took a look at some of the big picture beliefs of Christianity and how the evangelical spin many of us grew up with may have missed the mark, like engaging the Bible, the spiritual and physical implications of the gospel, the future God has planned, our commitment to doing the good of the kingdom, understanding what the church is, and facing suffering at the hands of insiders and outsiders. Then we gently strolled through what life together can look like as a community through examining the leadership of Jesus, our own spiritual authority, discipleship of the whole person, what it means to really worship, how our rituals keep us together, and what it looks like to invite people into our community.

But the journeys we undertook here are just the beginning—for me and for you. This could never be a comprehensive guide, but I hope you feel at peace as you walk into what's next for you, having walked with me through these destinations. And I hope you feel equipped to see God and the purpose of the people of God as a steady compass for the way.

The next leg of my journey has planned stops. I want to learn more from people of color (something I'm very aware is a gap in my education and my disentangling). And from ancient sources, like more of the church fathers and mothers in the first few centuries of Christianity, as much as new ones who point me to new discoveries that help me find beauty that leads to worship in every area of my life.

Maybe your journey will be the same, and maybe it won't. Maybe you need a rest before you join in again. Let's face it, it's uncomfortable and often painful. Don't be afraid of what you'll find or who you'll become along the way. Stripping away the old and finding what's underneath can often require processing complex history and emotions. I encourage you not to stop there—not to turn your faith into a museum. Like the walls, halls, and ceilings of the Hagia Sophia, wash away the dirt underneath the plaster, pull out your paints, and restore beauty that points you back to Jesus, to worship, and to wholeness.

Above all, friend, keep your eyes on the horizon. Resurrection day approaches. May that hope carry you through the journey ahead.

ACKNOWLEDGMENTS

MY BOOK, LIKE so many others, is the product of many years and the influence of many people.

First, I want to thank Daniel, my husband, for always being open to big talks and big dreams. I am grateful for the way we worked through all the changes we've undergone together, and that today, we're better people and better together than we've ever been.

My family is responsible for instilling in me a love for church and for the Bible. I wouldn't be able to write these words without their encouragement from the time I was young until today.

Thank you as well to Barb Roose, my agent, who took a chance on a girl with no credentials and a lot of opinions. Your guidance and partnership have been invaluable throughout this process.

I would like to thank AUMC for being a safe space to land when we weren't sure we would ever find a church.

I owe a debt of gratitude to Kristen Pool, Kat and Aaron Armstrong, and Seth Muse, who all called me up into my gifts and gave me spaces to use them. I know that without your belief in me back then, I would not be here now.

Dr. Caren Ferguson was my high school English teacher who told me I had a gift for writing and encouraged me to use it. Dr. Sandra Glahn was one of the first people to tell me that she thought I had something worth saying, and Mary DeMuth gave me the tools to get that something out into the world. Thank you all for being the cheerleaders I needed at each of those stages.

I need to thank Amanda and Christian Webb, our closest friends who sustained us in community in days filled with deep grief and who live out what it looks like to tangibly love your neighbor well.

I am grateful to Perkins School of Theology and especially my friends in the "Greek Squad." Y'all gave me the reassurance that there was a place for me in the church still and the community I needed in a season in which I unpacked a lot of hard moments and big beliefs.

Finally, this book would not have been possible without those who gave me the chance to go overseas and every person I encountered there. I don't know who or what I would be without those experiences, and I know my life, my faith, and my ministry are changed for the better because of each conversation. This book is a product of their influence. I stand here confidently because of their witness, and I hope I have done justice to their stories.

NOTES

Chapter 1

1 All names from overseas stories have been changed and their locations have been omitted for the security of the individuals involved.

2 "Deconstruction," *Encyclopedia Britannica*, https://www.britannica.com/topic/deconstruction.

3 Brian McLaren, "Emerging Values," *Leadership Journal*, July 1, 2003, www.christianitytoday.com/pastors/2003/summer/3.34.html.

4 John Franke, "Still the Way, the Truth, and the Life," *Christianity Today*, December 4, 2009, www.christianitytoday.com/ct/2009/december/6.27.html.

5 *The Wisdom Pattern* (Cincinnati, OH: Franciscan Media, 2020) is a good place to see a distillation of Rohr's thinking on all this.

6 Jen Hatmaker, "Fan Page Post," Facebook, April 23, 2016, www.facebook.com/permalink.php?story_fbid=946752262090436&id=203920953040241.

7 Justin Taylor, "Farewell Rob Bell?," *The Gospel Coalition*, October 30, 2017, www.thegospelcoalition.org/blogs/justin-taylor/farewell-rob-bell.

8 Tyler Huckabee, "The Evolving Faith of Lisa Gungor," *Relevant*, June 19, 2018, www.relevantmagazine.com/faith/the-evolving-faith-of-lisa-gungor.

9 Michael Gungor (@michaelgungor), "Thanks for all the thoughtful replies everyone. If you want to understand more of what I'm talking about, I would suggest 'Universal Christ' by Richard Rohr. Also, check out this season of the Liturgists podcast where we explore in depth how and why this tweet is true," Twitter, July 23, 2021, 11:25 p.m., https://twitter.com/michaelgungor/status/1418789361684992005.

10 Kurtis Vanderpool, "The Age of Deconstruction and Future of the Church," *Relevant*, April 7, 2021, www.relevantmagazine.com/faith/the-age-of-deconstruction-and-future-of-the-church.

11 Josh Harris (@harrisjosh), "My heart is full," *Instagram*, July 26, 2019, www.instagram.com/p/B0ZBrNLH2sl.

12 Patrick Manning, "What the Church Could Learn from Two YouTubers Losing Their Faith," *America Magazine*, November 17, 2020, www.americamagazine.org/faith/2020/11/17/deconstructing -christian-faith-rhett-link-youtube-catholic.

13 Carol Kuruvilla, "Evangelical Songwriter Says He's No Longer Christian in Emotional Instagram Post," *Huffington Post*, August 26, 2019, www.huffpost.com/entry/marty-sampson-hillsong -christianity-doubt_n_5d605421e4b02cc97c8d8724.

14 Carolyn Custis James, *Half the Church: Recapturing God's Global Vision for Women* (Grand Rapids, MI: Zondervan, 2010), 38.

15 "Mashiach, Mashach," *Brown-Driver-Briggs Hebrew and English Lexicon* (Peabody, MA: Hendrickson Academic, 1994), 603.

16 Walter A. Elwell, "Messiah," *Evangelical Dictionary of Theology*, 2nd ed. (Grand Rapids, MI: Baker, 2001), 764.

17 Elwell, "Messiah," *Evangelical Dictionary of Theology*.

18 Michael Svigel, "A Case for Retro Christianity," Credo House Ministries, May 9, 2009, https://credohouse.org/blog/a-case-for -retro-christianity.

Chapter 2

1 B. B. Warfield is an example of this kind of scholarly critic. He contributed to the Princeton theology on inerrancy we will discuss next. To understand his thoughts, see *The Inspiration and Authority of the Bible* (Phillipsburg, NJ: P & R Publishing, 1980). It elucidates the criticism of the "higher criticism" approaches to the Bible.

2 John R. Meuther, "The Fundamentalist-Modernist Controversy," *Tabletalk*, May 2020, https://tabletalkmagazine.com/article/2020/ 05/the-fundamentalist-modernist-controversy/.

3 Ernest Sandeen, *The Roots of Fundamentalism; British and American Millenarianism, 1800–1930* (Ada, MI: Baker Book House, 1978), 132–33.

4 Chicago Statement on Biblical Inerrancy, Article XII, https://www .moodybible.org/beliefs/the-chicago-statement-on-biblical -inerrancy/articles-of-affirmation-and-denial/.

5 Jonathan Merritt, "N. T. Wright on Homosexuality, Science, and Gender," *Religion News Service*, June 3, 2014, https://religionnews .com/2014/06/03/nt-wright-homosexuality-science-gender/.

6 Chicago Statement on Biblical Inerrancy, Article VI, https://www.moodybible.org/beliefs/the-chicago-statement-on

-biblical-inerrancy/articles-of-affirmation-and-denial/.

7   Michael Bird, *Seven Things I Wish Christians Knew about the Bible* (Grand Rapids, MI: Zondervan Reflective, 2021), 46.

8   For more on the Bible's authority and inspiration, see the books and websites of the following scholars: N. T. Wright, Tim Mackie, and Pete Enns.

9   Scot McKnight, "Inerrancy or Inerrancies?," *Scot's Newsletter*, June 1, 2021, https://scotmcknight.substack.com/p/inerrancy-or -inerrancies.

10 Bird, *Seven Things*, 44–45.

11 To learn more about and from Meredith Anne Miller, check out her podcast *Ask Away* and her Instagram @meredithannemiller.

12 For more on this, I recommend *The Blue Parakeet* by Scot McKnight (Grand Rapids, MI: Zondervan, 2018). He uses slightly different terms than I do for the pieces of the meta-narrative, but it shares many similar characteristics. He gives more time to the idea of story than I can here.

13 This became particularly noticeable in *The Second Apology* by Justin Martyr in paragraph 6.

14 Thomas H. Tobin, "Logos," *Anchor Yale Bible Dictionary* (New York: Doubleday, 1992), 347.

15 Leland Ryken, *How to Read the Bible as Literature* (Grand Rapids, MI: Zondervan Academic, 1985), and Kristie Anyabwile, *Literarily* (Chicago: Moody Publishers, 2022) are helpful tools for understanding the Bible's genres.

16 Some of my favorite resources for this information are the *Cultural Backgrounds Study Bible* (Grand Rapids, MI: Zondervan, 2016), the *New Interpreter's Study Bible* (Nashville: Abingdon Press, 2003), and the following websites: BibleHub.org, BibleProject.com, and NETBible.org.

17 A fun tool for seeing all the "y'all" in the text is yallversion.com. It translates "you" to "y'all" wherever the plural exists in the original languages.

18 Gary G. Porton, "Midrash," *Anchor Yale Bible Dictionary*, 820.

19 Ruth Graham, "As a 'Seismic Shift' Fractures Evangelicals, an Arkansas Pastor Leaves Home," *New York Times*, May 9, 2022, https://www.nytimes.com/2022/05/09/us/arkansas-pastor-evangelical -churches.html.

Chapter 3

1   Nicole Dungca et al., "A Dozen High-Profile Fatal Encounters That Have Galvanized Protests Nationwide," *Washington Post*, June 8,

2020, http://www.washingtonpost.com/investigations/a-dozen
-high-profile-fatal-encounters-that-have-galvanized-protests
-nationwide/2020/06/08/4fdbfc9c-a72f-11ea-b473-04905b1af82b
_story.html.

2 "Types of Justice," *Sociology Guide*, accessed 5/12/2021, http://
www.sociologyguide.com/weaker-section-and-minorities/Types
-of-Justice.php.

3 This is just one way to understand what happened in the atonement, called penal substitutionary atonement, and it is the most
common atonement theory among American evangelicals, which
is why I present it here. A helpful book on this subject, and why
you might need more than one atonement theory to understand
it, is Scot McKnight, *A Community Called Atonement* (Nashville:
Abingdon Press, 2007). If you're looking for a description of a few
specific atonement theories, see *The Nature of the Atonement: Four
Views*, edited by James Beilby and Paul R. Eddy (Westmont, IL:
IVP Academic, 2009), for a helpful summary.

4 "Dikaiosune," *Bible Dictionary of Ancient Greek* (Chicago: University of Chicago Press, 2000), 247–49.

5 You can look at the various replies here: https://twitter.com/
TheKateBoyd/status/1337442587578265600.

6 He makes this point often. One article adapted from a video
recorded around the time I heard that sermon is here: "Tony
Evans: God's Kingdom Demands Righteousness and Justice,"
Decision Magazine, July 1, 2020, https://decisionmagazine.com/
tony-evans-gods-kingdom-demands-righteousness-and-justice/.

Chapter 4

1 Kurt Rudolph, "Gnosticism," *Anchor Yale Bible Dictionary* (New
York: Doubleday, 1992), 1033–34.

2 Irenaeus's *Against Heresies* is a good resource for learning more
about Gnosticism and its rejection by the church among other
heresies.

3 Eric Weiner, "Where Heaven and Earth Come Closer," *New York
Times*, March 9, 2012, https://www.nytimes.com/2012/03/11/
travel/thin-places-where-we-are-jolted-out-of-old-ways-of-seeing
-the-world.html.

4 "Shalom," *Brown-Driver-Briggs Hebrew and English Lexicon* (Peabody, MA: Hendrickson Academic, 1994), 1022.

5 "Shalom," *Hebrew and Aramaic Lexicon of the Old Testament*
(Leiden: Brill Academic, 1994), 1506.

6 G. Gerleman, "Shalom," *Theological Lexicon of the Old Testament*,

vol. 3 (Peabody, MA: Hendrickson, 1994), 1340.

7 Lisa Sharon Harper, *The Very Good Gospel* (Colorado Springs, CO: WaterBrook, 2016), 43.

8 Michael J. Svigel, "Will God Annihilate the World?, Part II," *RetroChristianity,* May 20, 2009, http://www.retrochristianity.org/ 2009/05/20/will-god-annihilate-the-world-part-ii/.

9 W. Harold Mare, "Zion," *Anchor Yale Bible Dictionary* (New York: Doubleday, 1992).

10 M. S. Gignilliat, "Isaiah's Offspring: Paul's Isaiah 54:1 Quotation in Genesis 4:27," *Bulletin for Biblical Research* 25, no. 2, 216, https:// www.jstor.org/stable/26371272.

11 "Kosmos," *Bible Dictionary of Ancient Greek* (Chicago: University of Chicago Press, 2000), 561–62.

Chapter 5

1 John Wolffe and Richard V. Pierard, "Europe and North America," in Donald M. Lewis and Richard V. Pierard, eds., *Global Evangelicalism* (Westmont, IL: InterVarsity Press, 2014), 103.

2 Elle Hardy, "The 'Modern' Apostles Who Want to Reshape America Ahead of the End Times," *The Outline*, March 19, 2020, https://theoutline.com/post/8856/seven-mountain-mandate -trump-paula-white.

3 "What Is Christian Nationalism?" under "Learn More," Christians against Christian Nationalism, christiansagainstchristiannational ism.com.

4 N. T. Wright, "What Is a Working Model of the Kingdom of God?" video, https://www.facebook.com/watch/?v=206282850437614.

5 Mary Ann Getty-Sullivan, *Parables of the Kingdom* (Collegeville, MN: Liturgical Press, 2017), 7.

6 Walter A. Elwell, "Kingdom of Christ, God, Heaven," *Evangelical Dictionary of Theology*, 2nd ed. (Grand Rapids, MI: Baker Book House Co., 2001), 657.

7 Jonathan T. Pennington, *The Sermon on the Mount and Human Flourishing* (Grand Rapids, MI: Baker Academic, 2017), 155.

8 Friedrich Hauck, "Makarios," *Theological Dictionary of the New Testament* (Grand Rapids, MI: Eerdmans, 1967), 362.

9 Hauck, 366.

10 Amy-Jill Levine, *Sermon on the Mount* (Nashville: Abingdon Press, 2020), 8.

11 Levine, 17.

12 Evert Van De Poll, *Europe and the Gospel: Past Influences, Current Developments, Mission Challenges* (Warsaw: Sciendo, 2013), 261.

234/ AN UNTIDY FAITH

Chapter 6

1 J. Scott Duvall, *Experiencing God's Story of Life and Hope: A Workbook for Spiritual Formation* (Grand Rapids, MI: Kregel Academic, 2008), loc. 670–71, Kindle.

2 Walter A. Elwell, "Priesthood," *Evangelical Dictionary of Theology*, 2nd ed. (Grand Rapids, MI: Baker Book House Co., 2001), 952–53.

3 J. V. Fesko, "The Priesthood of All Believers," *The Gospel Coalition*, n.d., https://www.thegospelcoalition.org/essay/the-priesthood-of-all-believers/.

4 Skye Jethani, "The Evangelical Industrial Complex & the Rise of Celebrity Pastors," *Christianity Today*, February 2012, https://www.christianitytoday.com/pastors/2012/february-online-only/evangelical-industrial-complex-rise-of-celebrity-pastors.html.

5 David Brooks, "The Nuclear Family Was a Mistake," *The Atlantic*, March 2020, https://www.theatlantic.com/magazine/archive/2020/03/the-nuclear-family-was-a-mistake/605536/.

Chapter 7

1 Glen Harold Stassen, *A Thicker Jesus: Incarnational Discipleship in a Secular Age* (Louisville, KY: Westminster John Knox Press, 2012), 273.

2 *Lives of the Prophets* is an ancient account that compiles various oral and written traditions, put together during the apocryphal period, and is often given credit for the martyrdom stories of the prophets in the Hebrew Bible. There is a good summary in the *New World Encyclopedia* online at https://www.newworldencyclopedia.org/entry/Lives_of_the_Prophets.

3 Maxwell Staniforth and Andrew Louth, *Early Christian Writings* (Penguin Random House, 1968), 55.

4 Staniforth and Louth, *Ignatius' Letter to the Romans*, 84–85.

5 Staniforth and Louth, 86.

6 "St. Ignatius of Antioch," *Encyclopedia Britannica*, https://www.britannica.com/biography/Saint-Ignatius-of-Antioch.

7 Acts 11:26, *Cultural Backgrounds Study Bible* (Grand Rapids, MI: Zondervan 2016), loc. 165190–93, Kindle.

8 Staniforth and Louth, *Ignatius' Letter to the Romans*, 87.

9 James H. Cone, *The Cross and the Lynching Tree* (Maryknoll, NY: Orbis Books, 2011), 25.

Chapter 8

1 "Herodian Rulers," in *Encyclopedia of the Dead Sea Scrolls*, Lawrence H. Schiffman, James C. VanderKam, and Uriel Rappaport,

eds., *Oxford Biblical Studies Online*, November 5, 2020, http://
www.oxfordbiblicalstudies.com.proxy.libraries.smu.edu/article/
opr/t264/e213.

2 Raj Nadella, "The Two Banquets: Mark's Vision of Anti-Imperial
Economics," *Interpretation: A Journal of Bible and Theology* 70,
no. 2 (April 2016), 173.

3 Kate Shellnutt and Morgan Lee, "Mark Driscoll Resigns from Mars
Hill," *Christianity Today*, October 15, 2014, www.christianitytoday
.com/ct/2014/october-web-only/mark-driscoll-resigns-from-mars
-hill.html.

4 Daniel Silliman and Kate Shellnutt, "Ravi Zacharias Hid Hundreds
of Pictures of Women, Abuse During Massages, and a Rape
Allegation," *Christianity Today*, February 11, 2021, www.christian
itytoday.com/news/2021/february/ravi-zacharias-rzim
-investigation-sexual-abuse-sexting-rape.html.

5 Robert Downen et al., "20 Years, 700 Victims: Southern Baptist
Sexual Abuse Spreads as Leaders Resist Reforms," *Houston
Chronicle*, August 27, 2019, www.houstonchronicle.com/news/
investigations/article/Southern-Baptist-sexual-abuse-spreads-as
-leaders-13588038.php.

6 *The Jewish Annotated New Testament* (Oxford, UK: Oxford University Press), Kindle ed., 619–20.

7 *Jewish Annotated New Testament*, 621.

Chapter 9

1 Willie James Jennings, *Acts* (Louisville, KY: Westminster John
Knox, 2017), 86.

2 Jaime Clark-Soles, *First Corinthians: Searching the Depths of God*
(Nashville: Abingdon Press, 2021), 24.

3 Clark-Soles, *First Corinthians*, 25–26.

Chapter 10

1 Winfield Blevins, *Ever Ancient, Ever New* (Grand Rapids, MI: Zondervan, 2019), 206. I borrow the term *orthopathy* from Blevins and
others, but he would use it differently than I would. For him, liturgy
is the way of creating orthopathy or "right experience" that spiritually
forms, whereas I think of orthopathy as a descriptor of the "right
becoming" of a disciple who is healthy and whole, or strives to be.

2 A great resource for starting this work is *Emotionally Healthy Spirituality* by Pete Scazzero (Grand Rapids, MI: Zondervan, 2017). He
gives a number of tools within the book for the beginning of the
orthopathy journey.

3 John Burnet, *Early Greek Philosophy* (Veritatis Splendor Publications), loc. 5096, Kindle. Burnet provides an English translation of Heraclitus' fragments in chapter 3. The fragment quoted here is Fragment 119.

4 Joseph R. Myers, *The Search to Belong: Rethinking Intimacy, Community, and Small Groups* (Grand Rapids, MI: Zondervan, 2003), 30.

Chapter 11

1 Jaclyn Cosgrove, "L.A. Megachurch Pastor Mocks Pandemic Health Orders, Even as Church Members Fall Ill," *Los Angeles Times,* November 8, 2020, https://www.latimes.com/california/story/2020-11-08/la-pastor-mocks-covid-19-rules-church-members-ill. This is one example of several, but deserves attention for the size of the church and stature of its leader in many evangelical circles.

2 J. Scott Duvall, *Experiencing God's Story of Life and Hope: A Workbook for Spiritual Formation* (Grand Rapids, MI: Kregel Academic, 2008), loc. 642–43, Kindle.

3 J. Ramsey Michaels, *The Gospel of John, New International Commentary on the New Testament* (Grand Rapids, MI: Eerdmans, 2010), 251.

4 Jonathan Pennington, *The Sermon on the Mount and Human Flourishing* (Ada, MI: Baker Academic, 2017), 92.

5 "Nasa," *Brown-Driver-Briggs Hebrew and English Lexicon* (Peabody, MA: Hendrickson Academic, 1994), 669.

Chapter 12

1 This follows the general Baptist stance I grew up with and still maintain, which holds that baptism and communion are signs of the work done by Christ for our salvation and show our acceptance of that work, rather than as part of the work of salvation itself. This is by no means a comprehensive list, but some scriptures that have been used to uphold these stances on baptism are Matthew 28:19–20; Mark 16:16; Acts 2:38–39; 8:36; among others, which show believing in Jesus and baptism as separate entities—belief being the salvific act and baptism the physical sign of that act. For communion, some Scriptures to consider include Hebrews 9:25–28, which shows Christ's sacrifice of body and blood once were sufficient for all and need not be repeated, and 1 Corinthians 11:23–26, which positions communion as a remembrance and proclamation of the sacrifice of Christ until his return. If they are symbolic acts, then it follows that it is the faithful participation in

the rituals and not the elements or the rituals themselves that are efficacious. However, it should be stated that every denomination that holds a different stance also finds their evidence within Scripture, and these are arguably valid interpretations. What matters most is that baptism and communion are two rituals which we almost all agree are important to our Christian faith and practice.

2 Augustine of Hippo, *Homilies on the First Epistle of John* (CreateSpace Independent Publishing Platform, 2013), 202.

3 Michael C. McCarthy, "An Ecclesiology of Groaning: Augustine, the Psalms, and the Making of Church," *Theological Studies* 66, no. 1 (2005), 29–30, doi:10.1177/004056390506600102.

4 Gordon D. Fee, *The First Epistle to the Corinthians*, rev. ed., *New International Commentary on the New Testament* (Grand Rapids, MI: Eerdmans, 2015), 594.

5 I owe this phrasing to Melissa Florer-Bixler and a now deleted thread on Twitter. I wanted to give credit where it is due, however, and recognize this influence on how I speak about communion.

Chapter 13

1 Priscilla Pope-Levison, *Models of Evangelism* (Ada, MI: Baker Academic, 2020), 181.

2 Rick Richardson, *You Found Me* (Westmont, IL: InterVarsity Press, 2019), 9.

3 Richardson, *You Found Me*, 168.

4 Harvey Kwiyani, "Mission after George Floyd: On White Supremacy, Colonialism and World Christianity," *Anvil Journal of Theology and Mission*, October 2020, https://churchmissionsociety.org/anvil/mission-after-george-floyd-on-white-supremacy-colonialism-and-world-christianity-harvey-kwiyani-anvil-vol-36-issue-3/.

5 Stephen Neill, *Colonialism and Christian Missions* (New York: McGraw-Hill, 1966), 39.

6 Examples of this in early Christianity include the Ethiopian eunuch from Acts 8, the disciple Thomas, who is traditionally said to have taken the gospel to India, and even early church fathers who come from Africa, like Augustine.

7 Bartolomé de las Casas, *A Brief Accont of the Destruction of the Indies* (Seville, 1552; Project Gutenberg, 2007), 52, https://www.gutenberg.org/ebooks/20321.

8 William Carey's *An Enquiry into the Obligations of Christians to Use Means for the Conversion of the Heathens* is one such example of this language: https://www.wmcarey.edu/carey/enquiry/anenquiry.pdf.

9   Kwiyani, "Mission after George Floyd."

10 "American with No Medical Training Ran Center for Malnour-
    ished Ugandan Kids. 105 died," *All Things Considered*, August 9,
    2019, https://www.npr.org/sections/goatsandsoda/2019/08/09/
    749005287/american-with-no-medical-training-ran-center-for
    -malnourished-ugandan-kids-105-d.

11 "How Ethnic Minorities Can Experience Support Raising," Driving
    Diversity, "Resources" page, http://www.drivingdiversity.org/
    uploads/2/3/0/2/23029274/more_on_minority_support_raising
    .pdf.

12 Acts 6:5, *Cultural Backgrounds Study Bible* (Grand Rapids, MI:
    Zondervan, 2016), loc. 164592, Kindle.

THE AUTHOR

KATE BOYD IS a writer, speaker, and Bible teacher. She helps believers who find themselves in the messy middle between conservative and progressive navigate the tensions of the Christian life so they can more confidently walk the lines between doubt and certainty and faith and action with love and grace for all. She graduated cum laude with a BS in journalism and soon found her way to marketing and storytelling. She has traveled the world to interview and tell the stories of believers on mission, and she has written copy that has generated millions in revenue for nonprofits and small businesses. She is studying theology with an emphasis in church history and biblical languages at Perkins School of Theology.